The Liberal Lunacy

The New America And Her Problems

By

Danny Rossy

Copyright ©

Table of contents

When we say something is "political" or "all about politics," we usually mean that people or groups are fighting for power.The concept is that maneuvering to assert competing interests is the process of politics. Naturally, this idea of competing for power or interests is very important to party politics, or politics with a capital "P."In fact, we could begin by defining politics as the process of competing claims being made by opposing parties in order to garner support for these programs.Be that as it may, past this expansive definition, it's helpful to unload what's going on with this opposition and the manner by which it works out.These two inquiries will assist us in developing a somewhat nuanced (and hopefully less cynical!)perception of politics

First, what's the point of politics?The response that politics is about who gets what, when, and how is one of the most common ones to this question.According to this point of view, the primary goal of politics is to settle disputes regarding the distribution of tangible goods.This may have been a fair description of politics after World War II, when progressive taxation and welfare were implemented by a relatively centralized state and a party political system based on a traditional ideological divide between the left and right.

However, over the course of at least three decades, the idea that politics is solely or primarily about distribution has been questioned.Politics is as much, if not more, about identity and culture than it is about resources, according to the growing prominence of "post-ideological" debates over values and lifestyles.A lot of our contemporary political discussion spins around issues that are not conveniently sorted as left or right, like the climate, orientation and sexual freedoms, migration and security.

The "ideational turn" in political studies challenges this conventional view by arguing that political contestation is as much about cultural recognition and identity as it is about allocating resources.Scholars have demonstrated that disagreements over how to frame or describe policy issues are just as important to politics as conflicts over distribution.Of course, the two might be hard to tell apart:Problem framing approaches can have significant effects on distribution.But the point is that politics is a battle of ideas in which participants instead of invoking objective self-interest try to control the narrative by tapping into deeply ingrained values and beliefs.This acknowledgement of the significance of narratives coincides with discussions regarding "fake news" and the possibility of significant divergence in the ways in which opposing political groups frame policy issues.

The process of politics is the subject of the second question:How are these competing claims implemented in policy?The obvious response to this in multiparty democracies is to win elections, which allows parties to put their programs into action.

December 2019, MPs leaving the State Opening of Parliament.Adrian Dennis, WPA Pool, courtesy of Getty Images.

However, this transactional account is false.A "bidding war" in which rival parties promise ever more appealing programs is typical of electoral competition.As if they were choosing a product, voters frequently believe that these programs can be easily implemented.However, in reality, manifesto claims are frequently discarded or diluted in response to constraints on resources, viability, or political opposition.Democratic politics suffer as a result, causing disappointment and disappointment. Therefore, charting and comprehending these changes in the nature of politics is one of the challenges for political science.To make sense of the political disappointment caused by the gap between the transactional view and the messier reality, we must comprehend that political contestation is as much about cultural identity and recognition as it is about allocating material resources.We can only develop institutions capable of reviving democratic debate and political trust by elucidating these trends.No mean accomplishment in the ongoing political environment, yet certainly worth our maximum effort.

At the University of Edinburgh, Christina Boswell is Professor of Politics and Dean of Research for the College of Arts, Humanities, and Social Sciences.In 2019, she was made a Fellow of the British Academy.When we say something is "political" or "all about politics," we usually mean that people or groups are fighting for power.The concept is that maneuvering to assert competing interests is the process of politics. Naturally, this idea of competing for power or interests is very important to party politics, or politics with a capital "P."In fact, we could begin by defining politics as the process of competing claims being made by opposing parties in order to garner support for these programs.Be that as it may, past this expansive definition, it's helpful to unload what's going on with this opposition and the manner by which it works out.These two inquiries will assist us in developing a somewhat nuanced (and hopefully less cynical!)perception of politics

First, what's the point of politics?The response that politics is about who gets what, when, and how is one of the most common ones to this question.According to this point of view, the primary goal of politics is to settle disputes regarding the distribution of tangible goods.This may have been a fair description of politics after World War II, when progressive taxation and welfare were implemented by a relatively centralized state and a party political system based on a traditional ideological divide between the left and right.

However, over the course of at least three decades, the idea that politics is solely or primarily about distribution has been questioned.Politics is as much, if not more, about identity and culture than it is about resources, according to the growing prominence of "post-ideological" debates over values and lifestyles.A lot of our contemporary political discussion spins around issues that are not conveniently sorted as left or right, like the climate, orientation and sexual freedoms, migration and security.

The "ideational turn" in political studies challenges this conventional view by arguing that political contestation is as much about cultural recognition and identity as it is about allocating resources.Scholars have demonstrated that disagreements over how to frame or describe policy issues are just as important to politics as conflicts over distribution.Of course, the two might be hard to tell apart:Problem framing approaches can have significant effects on distribution.But the point is that politics is a battle of ideas in which participants instead of invoking objective self-interest try to control the narrative by tapping into deeply ingrained values and beliefs.This acknowledgement of the significance of narratives coincides with discussions regarding "fake news" and the possibility of significant divergence in the ways in which opposing political groups frame policy issues.

The process of politics is the subject of the second question:How are these competing claims implemented in policy?The obvious response to this in multiparty democracies is to win elections, which allows parties to put their programs into action.

December 2019, MPs leaving the State Opening of Parliament.Adrian Dennis, WPA Pool, courtesy of Getty Images.

However, this transactional account is false.A "bidding war" in which rival parties promise ever more appealing programs is typical of electoral competition.As if they were choosing a product, voters frequently believe that these programs can be easily implemented.However, in reality, manifesto claims are frequently discarded or diluted in response to constraints on resources, viability, or political opposition.Democratic politics suffer as a result, causing disappointment and disappointment. Therefore, charting and comprehending these changes in the nature of politics is one of the challenges for political science.To make sense of the political disappointment caused by the gap between the transactional view and the messier reality, we must comprehend that political contestation is as much about cultural identity and recognition as it is about allocating material resources.We can only develop institutions capable of reviving democratic debate and political trust by elucidating these trends.No mean accomplishment in the ongoing political environment, yet certainly worth our maximum effort.

At the University of Edinburgh, Christina Boswell is Professor of Politics and Dean of Research for the College of Arts, Humanities, and Social Sciences.In 2019, she was made a Fellow of the British Academy.

In the 19th and early 20th centuries, the Liberal Party and the Conservative Party were the two major political parties in the United Kingdom. By the end of the 19th century, it had formed four governments under William Gladstone, beginning as an alliance of Whigs, Peelites who supported free trade, and reformist Radicals.The party returned to government in 1905 and won a landslide victory in the 1906 general election despite being divided on the issue of Irish Home Rule.

The Liberal Party enacted reforms that established a fundamental welfare state during the reigns of Henry Campbell-Bannerman (1905–1908) and H. H. Asquith (1908–1916). Although Asquith was the party's leader, David Lloyd George was its most influential figure.Asquith's wartime role as coalition prime minister overwhelmed him, and Lloyd George succeeded him in 1916, but Asquith continued to lead the Liberal Party.The party was severely weakened by the split between Lloyd George's breakaway faction and Asquith's official Liberal Party. The Conservative Party eventually overtook Lloyd George's coalition government in 1922 and became increasingly in charge.The Liberals had been replaced as the Conservatives' main rival by the end of the 1920s by the Labor Party.After 1918, the Liberal Party fell out of favor and won only six seats in general elections by the 1950s.Its fortunes did not significantly improve until 1981, when it formed the SDP–Liberal Alliance with the Social Democratic Party (SDP), despite notable victories in by-elections.The Alliance won over a quarter of the vote in the 1983 general election, but only 23 of the 650 seats it contested.The Liberals and the SDP merged in 1988 to form the Social and Liberal Democrats (SLD), which were renamed the Liberal Democrats the following year after their share of the vote dropped below 23% at the general election in 1987.In 1989, the Liberal Party was reconstituted by a splinter group.

The philosopher John Stuart Mill, the economist John Maynard Keynes, and the social planner William Beveridge are prominent intellectuals who are associated with the Liberal Party.Henry William Massingham called Winston Churchill's Liberalism and the Social Problem, published in 1909, "an impressive and convincing argument," and it is widely regarded as the movement's bible.

Liberalism is a political doctrine that views the protection and enhancement of individual freedom as the primary political issue.Dissidents normally accept that administration is important to shield people from being hurt by others, yet they likewise perceive that administration itself can represent a danger to freedom.In his 1776 pamphlet Common Sense, American Revolutionary War pamphleteer Thomas Paine argued that government is, at best, "a necessary evil."Laws, judges, and the police are necessary to protect a person's life and liberty; however, their coercive power can also be used against the person.Therefore, the issue is coming up with a system that both grants the government the authority it needs to safeguard individual liberty and prevents those in power from abusing that authority.

When one asks whether this is the only thing the government can or should do for individual freedom, the issue becomes even more complicated.It is, according to some liberals, the so-called neoclassical liberals or libertarians.However, since the late 19th century, the majority of liberals have insisted that the powers of the government can both promote and safeguard individual freedom.Modern liberalism holds that removing obstacles that prevent individuals from living freely or from fully realizing their potential is the primary responsibility of the government.Discrimination, ignorance, poverty, and disease are examples of such obstacles.The conflict among nonconformists about whether government ought to advance individual opportunity as opposed to simply safeguard it is reflected somewhat in the different winning originations of radicalism in the US and Europe since the late twentieth 100 years.The welfare-state policies of the New Deal program implemented by the Democratic administration of President

Franklin D. Roosevelt, whereas in Europe, it is more commonly associated with adherence to laissez-faire economic policies and a commitment to limited government (see Contemporary liberalism below).

From the 17th century to the present, the political foundations and history of liberalism are discussed in this article.See political philosophy for coverage of classical and contemporary philosophical liberalism.For life stories of individual thinkers, see John Locke ;Mill, John Stuart;Jeremy Rawls

General characteristics Liberalism is based on two aspects of Western culture that are related.The first is the West's distraction with distinction, when contrasted with the accentuation in different developments on status ,

standing , and custom.People have been subordinate to their clan, tribe, ethnic group, or kingdom for a significant portion of history.The development of liberalism in Western society, which resulted in a realization of the significance of human individuality, a release of the individual from total subservience to the

group, and a loosening of the hold that custom, law, and authority had on society, is seen as the culmination of these developments.In this regard, liberalism represents individual liberation.Also see individualism.
In European political and economic life, liberalism is also derived from the practice of adversariality, or adversariness. In this process, institutionalized competition creates a dynamic social order, such as the competition between different political parties in elections, between prosecution and defense in adversary procedure, or between different producers in a market economy (see monopoly and competition).However, adversarial systems have always been unstable, and it took a long time for the belief in adversariality to emerge from the more conventional viewpoint, which can be traced back at least to Plato and holds that the state should be an organic structure similar to a beehive in which the various social classes cooperate by carrying out roles that are distinct but complementary.In the early 19th century, most European nations still held the odd belief that good government necessitates vigorous opposition and that competition is an essential component of a political system.
The conviction that human beings are fundamentally rational creatures capable of resolving their political disputes through dialogue and compromise lies at the heart of the liberal belief in adversariality.This part of radicalism turned out to be especially noticeable in twentieth century projects pointed toward dispensing with

war and settling conflicts between states through associations like the Class of Countries, the Joined Countries, and the Global Courtroom (World Court).

Access exclusive content with a subscription to Britannica Premium.

Subscribe Now The relationship between liberalism and democracy is close, but not always comfortable.The idea that governments are elected by the people is at the heart of democratic doctrine.On the other hand, the scope of governmental activity is the primary focus of liberalism.Therefore, liberals have frequently been wary of democracy out of concern that it might result in majority rule.As a result, one could swiftly assert that liberalism serves unpopular minorities while democracy serves majorities.

Liberalism, like other political doctrines, is extremely time- and circumstance-dependent.Liberalism varies from country to country and from generation to generation.Over the course of recent centuries, liberalism has progressed from a mistrust of the state's power due to its tendency to be misappropriated to a willingness to use it to correct perceived inequities in the distribution of wealth caused by economic competition— inequities that purportedly deprive some people of an equal opportunity to live freely.Liberals' desire for greater governmental power and accountability in the 20th century was clearly at odds with their earlier call for smaller government.Liberals were typically the party of business and the entrepreneurial middle class in the 19th century; however, for the majority of the 20th century, they were more likely to work to restrict and regulate business in order to expand opportunities for consumers and laborers.However, the liberals' motivation was the same in each case:a reluctance to reexamine and reform social institutions in light of new needs and a hostility toward concentrations of power that impede individuals' freedom and ability to achieve their full potential.The liberal and radical are distinguished from one another by their aversion to abrupt, cataclysmic change, which tempers this willingness.However, the liberal from the conservative, who believes that change is at least as likely to result in loss as it is to result in gain, is distinguished from the liberal by this very eagerness to welcome and encourage useful change.

THE NEED: A MASSIVE INFUSION OF STRATEGIC SUPPORT FOR U.S. DEMOCRACY

The state of American democracy is at a dangerous crossroads.The situation necessitates a significant shift in support and strategy.The country faces a democratic setback that could be as serious as the ones that are already taking place in India and Hungary, both of which are now only rated as "partially free" by Freedom House, and the nearly one hundred year reversal that occurred following the Reconstruction era in the United States.

Numerous Americans view this second with concern, however their concern is estimated:America's framework is creaky, however the world's most established vote based system has solid foundations and will get through.

However, since the end of the Cold War, elected governments have used legal means to undermine democracy, such as gerrymandering and technical rule changes, to the greatest extent.Their destruction of their own democracies has been backed by majority or plurality of their citizens, who are polarized and support policies that harm democracy to ensure their side wins.This is exactly where America is headed.

Resilience can be found in the United States' long history of democracy, but Americans shouldn't expect too much from the country's past.Due to a lack of precedent, many of the laws that create institutional guardrails were written poorly after the Civil War, containing easily contested loopholes.In addition, due to the country's age, a lot of what are thought to be laws and institutions are merely norms.These norms are rapidly deteriorating.

Already, other charitable organizations and individuals are aware of the danger America faces.In an effort to restore democracy, they are investing time and resources into increasing voter turnout, particularly among minorities and swing voters.These efforts are needed, but not enough.Despite the fact that record numbers of people, minorities, and swing voters voted, America's democratic decline has accelerated.Additionally, despite Democratic control of both chambers of Congress and the presidency at the national level, democratic decline in many states has accelerated for those on both sides of the aisle who believe these voting measures will save U.S. democracy.A more effective strategy is required by the support group for American democracy.

THIS PAPER HAS FOUR PARTS
The Danger:
International markers of American democracy's swift decline
The playbook already underway at the state level to undermine democracy
How polarization is enabling antidemocratic action
The rise in political violence against key, targeted groups
Five Strategies with concrete tactics to alter the current disintegration
Enable responsible conservatives to vote for democracy
Reduce the social demand from the right for illiberal policies and politicians
Engage the left in defending democracy by making it deliver
Build a broad-based, multi strand, pro democracy movement around a positive vision concretized in locally rooted action
Strengthen accountability to reset norms on what behavior is legal and acceptable
Insufficient Tactics: activities that are crucial to hold democratic ground but that will not alter the trajectory
Help Democrats win
Increase voter turnout
Get more minorities to vote
Court more swing voters

Improve election administration
Increase economic redistribution
Fix gerrymandering
Three Near-Term Futures:
Stable states run by one political party where voters cannot alter politics
States run by one political party whose control is upheld by violence
A political stalemate with increased criminal and political violence
America is in a vicious cycle, and it is speeding up. Severe polarization is rapidly narrowing the available solution sets. The moment is serious and dire.
Yet it is not hopeless. During the 1890s in an era known as the Gilded Age, which was the last period of polarization as vast as today's, America faced even greater troubles. Politicians were openly bribed, and legislation was bought. Company-controlled militias controlled their workers with tools such as an armor-plated vehicle mounted with machine guns known as the "death special" with legal support from the Supreme Court. Serious movements for communism and anarchism threatened the country's democratic foundations. Anarchist bombings and the assassination of a president elevated political violence. Meanwhile, as historian Robert Mickey explained:
Leaders of the eleven states of the Old Confederacy founded stable, one-party authoritarian enclaves under the "Democratic" banner. . . . These rulers curtailed electorates, harassed and repressed opposition parties, and created and regulated racially separate—and

significantly unfree—civic spheres. State-sponsored violence enforced these elements.

What followed was not the death of democracy. Instead, many Americans with different interests brought about social and political reforms that revitalized the social contract and enabled the so-called American Century of the 1900s. Unfinished work from that set of democratic changes led to the Civil Rights Movement.

We must act now, at scale, with strategy.

As political scientist Lee Drutman has written, a nadir can also enable a change of direction. Today, Americans have a chance to not just piece together the cracked remnants of what was—but to create the next chapter of America. In fact, we not only can do better, but we must think bigger to galvanize the movement we need to succeed at our immediate challenges. We must act now, at scale, with strategy.

THE DANGER: AMERICA'S DEMOCRATIC DECLINE
U.S. DEMOCRACY IS IN SWIFT DECLINE
The United States is in serious decline on every major international measure of democracy.Since 2010, the Index of Varieties of Democracy has been tracking the rise of autocracy;In 2017, the Economist Intelligence Unit lowered the status of the United States to that of a "flawed democracy;"The United States is now categorized as a "backsliding democracy" by Europe's International Institute for Democracy and Electoral Assistance;Additionally, Freedom House identifies the United States as having one of the countries' quickest

declines in democratic quality, ranking it third only to Croatia and Romania.

Over the course of more than two decades, America has struggled with democratic issues that have existed for a long time.Politics in the country have fundamentally changed, and many Americans who were born in previous decades are unaware of how significant the shift has been.Because so many states were in competition before the 1990s, the terms "swing" and "battleground" did not exist.Now, only a few are running for president, raising the stakes in those areas and effectively disenfranchising many voters whose votes in safe constituencies with a negative contra-majority are known to have little impact.The number of so-called safe seats, which now make up about 90% of the House of Representatives, has increased even more as a result of this year's redistricting.Candidates are forced to accommodate the viewpoints of extreme partisans because there are so many safe seats, rather than shifting to one side during primary elections and back to the middle during general elections.In the 1970s, a change was made to make the filibuster, a procedural tool that allows a minority of senators to halt legislation even if the majority supports it and requires sixty votes to override, easier to use.However, it has only been used frequently since 2010.It has transformed rule by the majority into rule by the supermajority, which has resulted in gridlock, increased incentives for gerrymandering, and dissatisfaction among Americans who believe that even voting for a party that wins the majority does not advance their policy objectives.

The doors to the urgent issues of today were opened by these slow-moving phenomena.Through polarization and safe seats, antidemocratic politicians have begun enacting an authoritarian strategy.Over the past five years, this strategy has significantly accelerated the breakdown of democratic institutions.Like the American creator Ernest Hemingway's popular jest about how one fails, America has been losing its majority rules system at first continuously, and afterward unexpectedly.

This lapse can be attributed in part to the left.In the section on strategies, I offer strategies for reversing the alienating politics of the left that are deepening polarization, preserving static identities, and fostering a sense of competitive victimhood, as well as leading many Americans toward extremism.However, there is asymmetrical rapid decline.It is primarily being driven by a Republican Party that is quite distinct.

Half of the Republicans who were present in Congress on the day that former president Donald Trump took office are no longer in office.About 75% of Republican House and Senate seats have changed hands since the Republicans' Tea Party revolution, a supposedly populist upsurge partially orchestrated from the top in 2008 to change the party's power structure.Those Republicans who have been more bipartisan or willing to stand up for democratic norms are leaving, including former congressmen Jeff Flake, Peter Meijer, and Rob Portman.Representatives Lauren Boebert, Madison Cawthorn, and Marjorie Taylor Greene are among those who were elected after 2008.Nearly all of those who are known to have requested preemptive pardons from

Trump for their role in the uprising were elected after 2008.The Republican Party's extremist wing is a recent development with already wide-ranging national and state-level reach.21% of Republican state legislators had joined extremist social media groups, according to a report by the Institute for Research and Education on Human Rights, a group that has long tracked white nationalism and anti-Semitism.This trend is being accelerated by Trump, but Trump's absence alone will not reverse the damage.

The Republican Party is no longer the party of former president Ronald Reagan or of conservatives like Representative Liz Cheney who have been in office for a long time.The current Republican Party appears much closer to authoritarian populist parties like the Justice and Development Party in Turkey and the Fidesz–Hungarian Civic Alliance in Hungary than to mainstream conservative parties like the Christian Democratic Union in Germany or the Conservative Party in Canada, according to a paper that categorizes over 1,000 political parties in 163 countries according to ideology and tactics.

That is on the grounds that heads of this new conservative group are further right as well as undeniably less dedicated to vote based foundations, practices, and standards.They are aware that their primary threat is from a primary challenger in seats that are becoming increasingly secure.A base of predominantly White, evangelical, rural men gained more formerly swing voters in 2016 who cared about identity issues but wanted more economic redistribution from the government than traditional conservative policy issues like low taxes or small government.These politicians have also reached political maturity when they realize that violence and voting manipulation will not be punished at the ballot box, despite the fact that bipartisanship can enable hit ads that hurt their chances in primaries.

A CORROSIVE PLAYBOOK IS ALREADY UNDERWAY
The democracy community needs speed and strategy at scale, because antidemocratic activity at the state level is already well underway. It is following a playbook pioneered by democracies that have been destroyed recently in other countries as well as in the United States' own past authoritarian enclaves.

Legal changes to alter who can vote, which votes count, and who adjudicates. In Hungary, the Fidesz party used autocratic legalism to legally alter laws with the support of voters until the playing field for democracy was irrevocably tilted in a way that created supermajorities for one party. President Viktor Orban, who was elected to a fourth term in 2022 despite the country's remaining six opposition parties backing a single candidate, shows how effective such legal manipulations can be.

In America, many states have been flooded with laws to alter voting. The worst of these maneuvers have occurred in a dozen states that have passed laws transferring power to more partisan electoral bodies and/or criminalizing their election administrations. These antidemocratic legal moves cannot be overcome by turnout.

For example, in Texas, poll watchers must be granted access to any part of a polling location. Texas has also criminalized any action by an election worker to restrain poll watchers. Texas also has an open carry gun law with no permit requirement. So, if poll watchers walked into a polling location with assault rifles in Texas, their actions may run afoul of federal intimidation legislation but appear to be in keeping with state legislation. A judge would have to adjudicate. Meanwhile, the law preventing election officials from intervening means that at best they can call law enforcement, whose presence can also have intimidating effects at polls.

At the same time, protective laws are failing. Michigan's secretary of state tried to pass what is known as a time-and-place ban, which would have restricted the open carrying of guns into or within 100 feet of polling stations during the state's early voting and election period in 2020. A judge blocked the effort. That ruling opened the door for what followed when Michigan gubernatorial candidate Ryan Kelley (whom the Federal Bureau of Investigation [FBI] would later arrest for egging on the crowd at the U.S. Capitol on January 6) and state senate candidate Mike Detmer met with poll workers in Michigan. Kelley suggested that those worried about fraud should unplug tabulation machines, while Detmer reportedly advised poll workers to "be prepared to lock and load. So, if you ask what we can do, show up armed."

Meanwhile, an obscure legal tactic could allow state legislatures to legally select their own slates of electors (whose votes are those that actually count to determine the winner of the presidency), regardless of the will of their voters. The "independent state legislature" theory argues that the Constitution gives state legislatures alone the final determination of election procedures, superseding state constitutions, courts, governors, and even voters, whose votes for electors are only advisory. This once-fringe theory sounds far-fetched, but the Supreme Court has taken a case that will allow it to decide on the theory in June 2023, and four of the sitting Supreme Court justices have previously indicated their potential support in decisions from Bush v. Gore (2000) to spring 2022. While Supreme Court Justice Amy Coney Barrett has remained silent, the activism of this Supreme Court does not encourage confidence.

A coordinated campaign with bureaucratic, electoral, and violent components is attempting to replace competent, long-standing election officials of both parties with partisan activists.

The democracy community should stop conflating these dire changes with measures that require voter identification or reduce mail-in ballot access. I address such laws in the "necessary but insufficient" section, because their results are mixed.

Personnel changes to ensure extreme partisans adjudicate election decisions. The key Republican in Wayne County, Michigan, who certified Detroit's election and thus allowed the state's votes to be counted, has since been replaced with a fierce election denier. Georgia's Republican secretary of state, who refused to look for the 11,000 votes that Trump asked him to find, has faced death threats, harassment, and a Trump-supported primary challenger (though he ultimately kept his seat). A coordinated campaign with bureaucratic, electoral, and violent components is attempting to replace competent, long-standing election officials of both parties with partisan activists.

Threats of violence against election workers, once nearly nonexistent, are now frequent—the Department of Justice (DOJ) has tracked over a thousand threats against election officials since the 2020 elections. In Colorado, threats are severe enough that some election officials are undertaking active shooter training and have been told to drive home following different daily routes to maintain their safety. A 2022 Brennan Center poll found that one in six election officials had experienced threats, and half had not reported them. About 50 percent had been threatened in person—not just online or on the phone. One in three knew at least one official who had already quit because of fear or threats.

The criminalization of routine electoral work is also part of a campaign to force out existing election workers and replace them with partisan activists. Laws are already being used in Arizona, Wisconsin, and elsewhere, forcing bureaucrats and bipartisan election boards to retain legal counsel to avoid jail for normal election decisions. For instance, in Arizona, new, contradictory laws forced the secretary of state to face criminal charges if she updated state election machines with the new maps. But these updates were also required by statute, following census-required redistricting. After updating them as required, she must now deal with the fear of jail time as a result. Many election workers are deciding that keeping their jobs is not worth these potential consequences.

America has the most decentralized elections in the world, and to run fair elections, local officials must master highly localized information and bureaucratic arcana. The median election official has worked in that role for twelve years; in large districts, most have served fifteen or twenty years. Fears of criminal, legal, or violent repercussions are creating an exodus of mid-level professional staff—the level of resignations since 2020 is unprecedented.

Stop the Steal activists—who wrongfully maintain that Trump won the 2020 U.S. presidential election—are being courted to replace them. Trump White House strategist Steve Bannon's podcast devotes an extra hour of programming each day to highlight the local officials he is recruiting to run for office. The United States has over 3,000 counties: an investigation of just sixty-five of them found 8,500 new Republican precinct officers, with no similar Democratic surge. These new officials are managing everything from voter registration to cybersecurity.

In addition to taking over professional staffing, election deniers are running for the top elected positions that manage state voting procedures. In Colorado, an election denier in charge of Mesa County's elections enabled voting machine passwords to be posted to public, online QAnon chat rooms. While she was indicted on ten counts by a Republican prosecutor, she is now running for secretary of state—a position that determines election rules. In fact, as of June 2022, two-thirds of those vying to be secretaries of state claimed that the 2020 election was fraudulent. More than one hundred election deniers have won their primary campaigns in 2022; nine states, including Michigan and Arizona, have election-denying candidates running for all major executive offices: governor, attorney general, and secretary of state.

This media echo chamber does not need to create a solid story that can be confirmed or denied. Instead, it is selling doubt.

Deepening doubt in elections as free and fair expressions of voter desires. Finally, just as Russian President Vladimir Putin has convinced many Russians that they are ridding Ukraine of Nazis, in the United States disinformation, misinformation, and malinformation on right-wing television and talk radio has succeeded in creating an alternate reality that facts cannot dislodge. This media echo chamber does not need to create a solid story that can be confirmed or denied. Instead, it is selling doubt. Voters who aren't sure that a particular form of wrongdoing happened, but simply feel that something is not right, are actually harder to persuade with facts. Thus, while in October 2020 solid majorities of Republicans believed elections were fair, months of conspiracy theory coverage by mainstream-right outlets means that now, only 35 percent trust the election system and nearly three-fourths believe the current president occupies the White House illegally.

These conspiracies build on one another. If you do not believe that COVID-19 is a serious disease, then altering election rules to make it easier to vote by mail in 2020 appears suspect. If you are concerned about an elite ring of pedophiles, then Democratic politicians requiring every American to wear a mask in public and establishing unprecedented lockdowns, which were widely reported to accelerate child abuse, appear pernicious. The building of conspiracy upon conspiracy—well-understood in psychological literature—makes unraveling each more difficult.

POLARIZATION CREATES VICIOUS CYCLES THAT ACCELERATE DISINTEGRATION

Much of the authoritarian playbook is unknown to voters. Polarization has allowed this authoritarianism into U.S. politics and enabled the sudden, rapid decline of U.S. democracy.

Polarization is based on some misbeliefs about the other side—which are greater among educated, media-consuming partisans on both sides and highest on the left. It is exacerbated by misinformation and disinformation. But it is also grounded in justified fears of the other side's social and policy agendas. The extreme level of U.S. polarization means that when the left describes its concerns about growing authoritarianism, the right has its own examples to list in return. Coronavirus-related mask mandates, lockdowns, and forced business and school closures mean that people on the right not only fear authoritarianism in the social and economic spheres but have had concrete, daily experiences with what many feel to be the curtailment of their democratic rights. The feeling that their fears of democratic loss have been dismissed by the left make it hard for the average conservative to take the left's concerns seriously. For instance, many felt a double standard when their economic, social, or mental health concerns about pandemic bans on public gatherings were ridiculed, while mass gatherings for Black Lives Matter protests were lauded. And while political violence and spontaneous hate crimes that harm people are being committed vastly more by those on the right and the overwhelming majority of Black Lives Matter protests were peaceful, the property damage from the few protests that were not resulted in over $2 billion in insurance payouts across twenty states, by far the most costly civil disturbance in modern U.S. history. The failure of the left to take such property losses and their personal costs—particularly to small business owners—seriously, and the conflation of these concerns with racism, galls many on the right.

Meanwhile, instances of mass shootings, school shootings, the sending of child services to the homes of parents of LGBTQ children, and the rollback of legal abortion even in some cases of rape, incest, and the health of the mother are handing people on the left daily, concrete losses of rights in an equally personal and visceral manner.

As policy agendas have become more extreme with less overlap over the last twenty years, partisans fear the other side so much that voters are willing to allow antidemocratic action by their side to keep the other out of power. By February 2021, 72 percent of each party was claiming the other was "a serious threat to the United States and its people."

Scholars Milan Svolik and Matthew Graham have found that 85 to 90 percent of U.S. citizens would vote for their party even if it engaged in undemocratic action, rather than across party lines. Numbers are far worse in states where voters have actually had to make such choices. A recent Bright Line Watch survey found that 28 percent of Democrats and 39 percent of Republicans favored "doing everything possible to prevent the other party from governing effectively"—numbers that reduced only slightly when misbeliefs about the other party were corrected.

Looking at cases of severe polarization globally since 1950, researchers Jennifer McCoy, Murat Somer, and Benjamin Press found that no other established democracy has been this polarized for as long as the United States. In McCoy's and Press's words,

There are no peer analogues for the United States' current political divisions—and the track record of all democracies does not provide much consolation."

The lack of consolation is because among less-established democracies that faced pernicious polarization, the majority experienced democratic degradation. Of the twenty-six countries that degraded, twenty-three descended fully into authoritarianism. Of the minority of cases that did not degrade, all but nine repolarized in ensuing years.

Polarization is allowing authoritarianism to take hold with voter support.

Globally, the world is in the sixteenth year of democratic recession. Democracies have primarily been dying at the hands of their own voters, who appreciate democracy but fear the other party so much that they will allow antidemocratic action to keep their side in power.

This is what is happening in America. Polarization is allowing authoritarianism to take hold with voter support.

METHODOLOGY

Attacks by far-left groups like anarchists and attacks that are partisan or support left-related policies like economic redistribution fall under the "far left" category.It includes attacks on law enforcement that are motivated by concerns about race or the left.Environmental terrorism, which encompasses animal rights and was significant enough to warrant its own subcategory, may be thought to be associated with the far left.Attacks that are partisan or support policies associated with the American right, such as anti-gun control, are included in the "far right" category. Other examples of groups associated with the far right include white supremacists, QAnon, and militias.Although they may be considered related to the far right, anti-abortion attacks were significant enough to warrant their own category.Hate-motivated terrorism against religious, ethnic, and racial minorities that cannot be linked to an organization is an example of anti-inclusivity.In the United States, the single-issue category includes individual attacks, terrorism linked to nonpartisan conspiracy theories, attacks motivated by personal motives, and other smaller categories that are not clearly associated with the right or left.

Attacks by individuals who are associated with al-Qaeda, the self-proclaimed Islamic State, or similar causes are included in the international/Hirabist category.Terrorism in which neither the motivation nor the identity of the perpetrator are known falls under this category.It primarily consists of unidentified bombings of White-majority Protestant, Catholic, and other churches as well as disturbed individuals' actions that do not appear to be influenced by a political ideology.

The author developed and coded these categories using data from the Global Terrorism Database (GTD).The GTD's event-based data set employs a definition of terrorism that excludes state violence and law enforcement-related violence.Additionally, it excludes spontaneous clashes at protests, riots, and more violent hate crimes.Ideological violence at protests and riots is included in the Armed Conflict Location & Event Data Project (ACLED) data set, but because it only started tracking U.S. data in 2020, it cannot show trends.However, the GTD data set and ACLED's existing data share a similar ratio of left- and right-wing violence.

A University of Chicago study found that nearly 10% of Americans agreed that "force is justified to restore [Trump] to the presidency" in the fall of 2021.A separate survey of 22,900 people found that nearly one in five Republican men believed violence could be justified "right now."Hate crimes have been reported by the FBI to their highest level since the backlash against Muslims that followed the terrorist attacks of September 11, 2001.Since 2017, white supremacist propaganda has nearly doubled, and supremacists are holding three times as many public events.

On the left, violent desires are also expanding.According to data from the Global Terrorism Database, there has been a slight increase in attacks, particularly against law enforcement and prominent Trump supporters.According to a survey conducted in February 2021 by Nathan Kalmoe and Lilliana Mason, 11% of Democratic respondents supported the assassination of opposition politicians.According to a July 2022 survey of over 8,000 people, 36% of those who supported violence in defense of ethnic or racial minorities were those who supported political violence.Meanwhile, threats directed at congressional members from both parties are more than ten times higher than they were five years ago:Capitol Police investigated 5,206 threats in 2018, up from 902 in 2016 and 3,939 in the first year of Trump's presidency;8,613 in 2020;and 9,625 in 2022. Aside from the immensely unbalanced number of occurrences, there is one more vital distinction among left-and conservative viciousness from a majority rule government stance.

On the left, those who advocate violence are least likely to identify with the Democratic Party, indicating a disillusioned segment over whom the Democratic Party does not have control.

People on the right who support violence the most strongly identify with the Republican Party.Because of this, they can use violence to achieve political objectives.In 2016 and 2018, right-wing post-election violence and intimidation began to coincide with the political calendar.By 2020, key election procedure dates were strongly associated with armed demonstrations and violence.In other words, right-wing violence and intimidation are targeted.

Consequently, many individuals do not perceive this rise in violence.They consider the uprising on January 6 to be an isolated incident.It isn't, though.The political use of violence, threats, and intimidation on the right serves three purposes.

1.to create a single Trumpist-Republican-Conservative identity by intimidating pro-democracy Republican politicians and thought leaders, forcing them to resign or silence themselves.

Fierce strategies are being utilized against conservatives who show popularity based spine to wipe out the choice of being a pro democratic, moderate conservative or a conservative who participates in bipartisanship.Due to the persistent harassment and threats of violence directed at him, his wife, and their young children, Representative Adam Gonzalez, one of the Republicans who voted to impeach Trump following January 6, has decided not to run for reelection.Trump declared, "1 down, 9 to go!" shortly after his announcement.Four of the ten Republicans who voted for Trump's impeachment are retiring; two of them have acknowledged that they were threatened with death.In fact, threats and violence, frequently with the participation of militias, have been directed at nearly

every Republican decisionmaker at the national or state level who supported free and fair elections in 2020.
A number of colleagues admitted receiving death threats after Marjorie Taylor Greene doxed them for supporting the infrastructure bill sponsored by U.S. President Joe Biden.Frank Upton, a retiring Republican who voted for Biden's infrastructure bill and Trump's impeachment, acknowledged that the death threats, particularly against his spouse and family, were frightening and would affect the willingness of other representatives to vote for measures sponsored by the opposing party to create bipartisan legislation.Out of public service, parents may be particularly vulnerable to intimidation.After being singled out by Trump and receiving threats so significant that his children were given protection by Philadelphia police, Republican election board member Al Schmidt quit.
Local Republican parties are also being overthrown by violent organizations.The Proud Boys, a right-wing, European chauvinist group, participated in crucial Nevada votes to sideline pro-democracy Republicans and empower a more Trump-aligned faction, allegedly at the direction of state Republican leadership. Clark County is the seat of Las Vegas and the state's largest county.Local leaders canceled other gatherings in an effort to avoid being removed from office and scheduled meetings in schools precisely because they were gun-free zones.Additionally, Proud Boys have joined the Miami-Dade County Republican Party's leadership, transforming meetings into intimidating shouting matches and driving traditional conservatives away.

Opinion leaders are another target.They pose a serious threat to the antidemocratic group by offering a conservative and pro-democratic option.Many well-known conservative media figures, like evangelical journalist David French, have received death threats and threats against their families, which has discouraged other members of the conservative establishment from speaking out in favor of democracy and following in their footsteps.Free speech can be silenced through violence.Violence also contributes to polarization because it reduces the marketplace of ideas to a binary of antidemocratic Republicans or Democrats.

2.To take out authorities who disrupt the general flow of taking a future political race.

Similar strategies are being employed against elected and administrative election officials from both parties to thwart efforts to modify rules or procedures that would make it possible to steal a future election.There have been attacks on the homes of state secretaries like Jocelyn Benson of Michigan, Katie Hobbs of Arizona, Jena Griswold of Colorado, and Maggie Toulouse Oliver of New Mexico.Throughout the election season, some were forced to relocate.Temporary election workers and staff at the mid-level have also been targeted.

Bill Gates in Maricopa County, Arizona, a Republican state and county official, falls into the first category as well as this one and is thus targeted for both reasons. He has advocated for democracy and the fairness of their elections.

3.to strengthen the base by identifying perceived enemies against which to unite and appealing to a common identity.

Base voters, whose grievances unite them but do not always share the policy beliefs of traditional conservative constituencies, are united by the use of dehumanizing language and increasingly violent imagery against women, minorities, and Democrats. This dehumanization may include vile racial epithets, violent misogynistic imagery, and jokes that employ similar dehumanizing tropes, as well as accusations that Democratic politicians, school board members, and community leaders are "groomers" for pedophilia.All of these tactics cause supporters who are more aggressive to threaten, dox, and occasionally use actual violence against Democrats;religious, racial, and ethnic minorities;and females.

An attempt to unite and intensify base voters resulted in these forms of violence.As a result, they are the most common form of violence and threats, affecting mayors and members of Congress as well as members of school boards.At the local level, where municipalities lack the resources to safeguard officials, threats are multiplying:A survey conducted prior to the increase in threats in 2020 found that 13% of mayors had experienced physical violence.Health departments, school boards, and other institutions are facing even more violence and threats as a result of extremist groups like the Proud Boys piggybacking on mainstream right-wing targets.

Women, particularly minority women, are three times more likely to be targeted.Intimidating and abusive messages were sent to Democratic female politicians ten times more frequently than to their male counterparts, with minority women being the most frequently targeted.However, it also has an impact on immigrants, minorities, and everyday women through an increase in hate crimes and mass shootings.Despite the fact that this type of violence is more about uniting the base than it is about harming the target, it fosters efforts to target Black female poll workers and other members of these denigrated communities who fall into the first or second categories.

Violence is more reminiscent of the 1960s and 1970s on the left:It is coming from outside the system, from fringe individuals and groups fighting regular politics and acting haphazardly. Examples include the Bernie Sanders supporter who shot at Congress members during a baseball game and the young progressive men who attack police officers in the belief that they are supporting minority rights.However, far-left violence is on the rise and could get worse if prominent progressives start advocating for more violent views. The mainstreaming of violence is one of the most worrying aspects of the right.The majority of Americans who spontaneously commit hate crimes share demographic characteristics with other violent criminals:They are typically young men who have never been married, have no children, are unemployed, and frequently have prior criminal records.To put it another way, people who have a naturally aggressive personality and are likely to commit other violent crimes are motivated by the acceptance of hate to target people who are more involved in politics.

However, the majority of those who engage in organized political violence, such as on January 6 or at Stop the Steal events, are married, middle-class, middle-aged men who have children, work, and are involved in community or church groups.The majority of those arrested for the January 6 insurrection read mainstream media, not far-right echo chambers or social media.However, many were also members of extremist organizations.This well-established American community, in contrast to those who spontaneously commit hate crimes, appears to view violence and intimidation as an extension of their political voice or even an act of citizenship rather than as a criminal or terrorist act.

That is the final and most pressing reason for a shift in focus:It will probably get worse and be much harder to stop the violence that is now commonplace.

FIVE STRATEGIES TO CHANGE THE TRAJECTORY AND IMPROVE AMERICAN DEMOCRACY

America's democracy faces two very different problems. An acute threat is emanating from a faction of Republican politicians who are trying to gain control over the government to maintain power by reducing democracy. Their efforts build on long-term, slow-growing threats: a right where too many moderate conservatives are willing to support an antidemocratic faction to fend off the feared left, and a left where too many Americans aren't sure they care enough about the democratic system of government to fight for it.

Today's acute threats were able to metastasize quickly because society's immune system had been weakened by these long-term problems of polarization and decades of lost faith that democracy can deliver a better life. Thus, it isn't enough to restore the status quo from just before the acute threat took hold—Americans must use this crisis to propel their country forward.

Some of these tactics are short term, while others will take longer to come to fruition. All are difficult, but many have been achieved in countries far more violent and politically volatile than the United States is today.

However, waiting on the long-term goals and prioritizing the immediate will not succeed. The U.S. and NATO war in Afghanistan demonstrated how fighting twenty years' worth of one-year battles is a failing strategy.

Democracy proponents risk fighting endless two-year battles each election cycle, to equally failed results.

Instead, addressing the acute threats requires attention to both electoral and social

drivers (see table 1). I recommend five strategies:

1. enable responsible conservatives to vote for democracy,

2. reduce social demand from the right for illiberal policies and politicians,

3. engage the left in defending democracy by making it deliver,

4. build a broad-based, multi strand, pro democracy movement around a positive vision concretized in locally rooted action, and

5. strengthen accountability to reset norms on what behavior is legal and acceptable.

ENABLE RESPONSIBLE CONSERVATIVES TO VOTE FOR DEMOCRACY

With antidemocratic, illiberal politicians in charge, a democracy cannot exist.Over a third of Republicans are of the opinion that the elections in 2020 were free and fair.If that third person voted for Democrats and pro-democracy candidates, the United States would look like many European nations, where a small minority of irate voters support fringe parties rather than an existential threat to democracy.However, mainstream conservatives simply cannot bear to support Democrats, so pro-democracy Republican voters continue to fuel an anti-democracy faction of their party by winning Republican primaries.This is unlikely to change for identity and policy reasons:Split-ticket voting is becoming increasingly uncommon, negative partisanship is extremely high, and Republican voting has not changed significantly in response to antidemocratic tactics.

Additionally, electoral outcomes will not be affected by social strategies like building bridges.There is absolutely no evidence that changing a person's beliefs about other groups, such as making them feel more comfortable with immigrants or their social status, will change how they vote.Therefore, none of the subsequent social changes have the capacity to influence voting behavior in a manner that will save the country's democracy unless immediate electoral and longer-term institutional changes enable moderate Republicans to vote for pro democracy Republican candidates against an antidemocratic faction.

In the primary and general elections, back pro-democracy candidates to ensure that antidemocratic candidates lose and pro-democracy politicians from all parties win.Opportunistic politicians will continue to support illiberalism and antidemocratic tropes if antidemocratic candidates win because they see this as a winning election strategy, regardless of whether they agree with what they say.Even if they just say things that they don't actually agree with, leaders will still contribute to this vicious cycle because they have a lot of power to set social norms.

For that strategy's sake, candidates who spread antidemocratic or violent imagery or rhetoric must pay electoral costs.While tactically distinct, making certain that the gallant politicians from both parties who supported democracy in 2020 win is equally important.Both are crucial in shifting momentum.In addition to requiring innovative strategy, this suggestion necessitates campaign funding:In Utah, for example, the Democratic Party is supporting an independent, pro-democracy candidate who has a chance rather than running its own candidate in a state with a lot of conservatives.

These efforts in the short term are crucial.They also don't end.To maintain the line, they require significant expenditures every two years:for instance, the 2020 decisions cost $14 billion for public missions alone, not including races for state councils, lead representatives, and secretaries of state.Institutional reform is also required to address the problem's underlying causes. Advocacy for primary election reformFighting the antidemocratic faction is like trying to stop water from flowing through a sieve if there aren't changes to the institutions.Safe seats force all candidates to cater to a more extreme base, which means that in some elections, there won't be a clearly pro-democratic candidate to support—every viable candidate might question whether the 2020 election is legitimate.Over 90% of Congress members now vote in primaries because so many seats are now secure.Because of this, the Country First movement led by Representative Adam Kinzinger acknowledges that the campaign to elect pro-democracy Republicans cannot proceed without primary reform.

Within the two-party field, various forms of electoral change or majority-winner rules would permit what amounts to a multiparty system, allowing candidates from the same party to compete against one another without being spoilers.Changes like these include:ranked choice voting, in which voters rank several candidates in order of preference, and final-four or final-five voting, in which politicians from the same party can compete against one another, are examples of nonpartisan and open primaries, in which voters do not need to register with a party to vote, as well as ranked choice voting.Fusion voting, in which small parties like the Greens and Working Families Party can cross-endorse, proportional representation, and other systemic innovations are additional primary election reforms. In proportional representation, the number of seats held by a political party is proportional to the vote for the party in that area, rather than a single candidate winning the entire jurisdiction by winning 50%+1 votes.All of these changes make it possible for conservatives to vote pro-democracy without being seen as spoilers or throwing away votes.Partisans would be able to vote for pro-democracy candidates from their party thanks to these kinds of systemic innovations, which ought to differ from state to state.In areas where only one party is in power, these innovations would also make it possible for a larger number of voters to voice their opinions.

The 2020 elections for Cawthorn, Greene, and Boebert were decided by 5%, 8.3%, and 10.3% of their respective electorates, respectively, due to safe seats.However, Cawthorn lost the Republican primary in 2022 by 1,500 votes due to open primaries, which attracted at least 5,400 Democrats to cast ballots.Under Georgia's open primary system, Brad Raffensberger received over 37,000 votes from Democrats, giving him the 27,000 votes he needed to avoid a runoff. Cawthorn's outbursts against Republican colleagues and poor constituent services weakened his support for institutional reform, which is not a magic bullet that can overcome having a real majority due to popularity and funding.Greene, on the other hand, won her primary in part because she raised $9 million while the next most viable Republican had raised just over $390,000. Boebert, on the other hand, won her primary despite the fact that thousands of Democrats registered as

Republicans.Nonetheless, providing pro-democracy candidates with a fighting chance necessitates giving voters more choice and agency.Additionally, it increases trust in the system and representation.Moderation won't always come from it; as QAnon and election denialism grow, it might let immoral leaders win in some places.This is a recommendation that has both crucial importance and an expiration date, but the sooner primary reform is implemented and the more attention paid to the specific type of system in a given state, the less likely it is that these harmful effects will take hold.It must begin right now.

Establish a new persona for conservative Republicans to represent pro-democratic ideals.It is not sufficient to have an institutional means of voting for a conservative pro-democracy candidate in order to break the connection between a party and an illiberal social movement.For a regular voter, candidate, or public official to avoid being portrayed as a "Republican in name only" (RINO) for supporting democracy, a brand, identity, and social group must also exist.

As with Liz Cheney, who lost her primary, conservatives have been shamed, shunned, and punished when they have stood up for democratic principles one at a time.Jeff Flake, a former senator who decided not to run for office;and Cindy McCain, who was slammed by her own party and was a former Arizona Republican kingmaker as well as the wife of the late senator and former Republican presidential candidate John McCain.People who have publicly detested Trump, or Never Trumpers, have lost friends, jobs, and even places of worship.A movement with such high personal costs for such abstract goals attracts few people.All groups, and especially personalities with a tendency toward authoritarianism, are strongly influenced by social norms.

A permission structure for altering social norms can be created by creating a large, strongly identified conservative, pro-democracy group that people can identify with and belong to without fear of social rejection.Although it may be supported by a number of such organizations, the grouping must be a movement and not an official nongovernmental organization. Additionally, it must be large enough to thwart attempts to assassinate prominent figures one by one.In order for institutional reforms to produce value, this identity is necessary.

REDUCE SOCIAL DEMAND FROM THE RIGHT FOR ILLIBERAL POLICIES AND POLITICIANS

Address the status loss and dignity deficit that is driving some Americans to turn against democracy. The widespread feeling that the system is rigged, and that this intentionally tilted playing field has caused a once-privileged group to lose status (a feeling particularly strong among white Christian males), has opened a window for anti democrats to empathize and offer explanations that boost their power. America cannot have a healthy democracy without addressing these social forces.

Racism is clearly playing a dominant role in these dynamics, according to a multitude of studies. The problem, however, is intersectional. Beliefs about the properness of male dominance were more potent than racial beliefs in predicting whether men and women in 2016 and 2020 voted for Trump. Hostile sexism predicts support for political violence better than racism does. In both cases, however, there is correlation between these views and hostility toward people who are not white. Meanwhile, as Duke University political scientist Ashley Jardina has shown, mobilized white identity politics transcends class. So does hostile sexism. Plenty of college-educated White men (and some of the women who love them) feel their relative loss of status to minorities and women perhaps even more keenly, because they expect to be in the top place on the social spectrum. But class still plays a role: American men and women without college degrees hold more traditional views on gender, religion, and other issues. Today's culture wars sideline economics in order to unite non-college-educated Americans with many White people, men, and working class or male minorities, particularly Hispanics who may hold more traditional religious beliefs and gender norms.

To many American liberals, this may feel like the perfect moment for a comeuppance. But the impulse to rub White male noses in their perceived status loss plays right into the hands of authoritarians.

The weaponization of cultural issues is allowing what had been social divisions in the culture wars of the 1960s and partisan divides in the culture wars of the 1980s to fuel an authoritarian movement today.

Political organizers build political identity around a "story of self, a story of us, and a story of now," in pioneering community organizer Marshall Ganz's words—or, as Ian Haney López writes, who we are, what status we hold, who validates us, and who threatens us. Recognizing that men, White people, Christians, and working-class Americans are all grappling with their relative loss of status over the past fifty years, an antidemocratic faction has woven a successful narrative. Soft and sometimes explicit versions of the so-called great replacement theory claim that White people, men, and Christians are being displaced from their positions by minorities, women, and immigrants who are being let into the country or elevated to power by Democrats, Jews, "the government," or "elites." The QAnon claims of blood-drinking, satanic pedophiles supported by a "deep state" sound crazy, but they are actually a version of this story—one that paradoxically appeals less to self-interest and more to the helper impulse by saying that Christian childrens' souls are under threat from Democratic elites who hold cultural and political power. With stakes so high, democracy must be curtailed to save Christianity, White people, and men or, in a softer version, the Christian-European heritage that has made America great.

The story explains why some groups are losing status, validates some individuals' difficulty competing, and provides immediacy to antidemocratic efforts to keep other Americans permanently away from power. But the Trumpist faction of the Republican Party offers more than ideology. Like any good organizing effort, it also provides understanding and community, potent offerings in an age where anomie and loneliness are at alarming levels.

The weaponization of cultural issues is allowing what had been social divisions in the culture wars of the 1960s and partisan divides in the culture wars of the 1980s to fuel an authoritarian movement today.

The authoritarian movement is cultivating a story that puts men, Christians, and White people at the top of a status hierarchy. The pro democracy community must remain inclusive and liberal—but writing off all members of these groups as racist or unsaveable simply thrusts them closer together. Instead, the democracy movement must understand how this story brings out the worst in many individuals who also have better selves. Rather than pushing them to bond further with the authoritarian movement, it is crucial to separate allies from within these groups who will support inclusive democracy. That sounds unappealing to many who wish to write off much of America and move forward without them. But if pro-democracy efforts don't reach people who are feeling their loss of status and seeking explanations, then authoritarian politicians, male-chauvinist Proud Boys, incel chat boards, hypermasculine militia movements, and myriad white nationalist groups are happy to recruit them instead.

Once a status hierarchy is created, it is not just those at the top who maintain it. People tend to make their most socially respected identity the most salient. Therefore, some middle- and working-class men tie themselves to a higher rung by emphasizing their whiteness. Hostile sexism is also common among women, many of whom hold onto ideas of rightful male dominance and anti-female attitudes to raise their status within the right-wing hierarchy. The population with the greatest support for anti-Semitic views are young conservative Latino men, and second highest is young conservative Black men. But not all those who support a traditional hierarchy are trying to put others down. For some working-class families facing the brutal realities of raising kids while one parent works a morning shift and the other has shift work at night, attaining traditional stay-at-home motherhood is a mark of success and family stability. These families resent elites with choices for sneering at a goal they hope to someday achieve. Minority men and immigrants may emphasize their identity as hard-working and law-abiding or focus on their work identities as small business owners, and they may not want to share their hard-fought gains with others whom they don't feel followed the same rules. For instance, Pew Research Center found that 19 percent of Latino people favored Trump's border wall in 2018, a figure that rose to 48 percent among Latino conservatives. One in ten African Americans today are immigrants and may identify more with gender norms from their home countries, or with a story of immigrant striving, than with the struggle against American racism. Others may feel their masculinity or religious beliefs are more important to them than their race or ethnic identity and may support traditional, but not hostile, relationships with women.

The fact that people have many identities to choose from helps explain why the Hispanic vote for Trump increased by over a third between 2016 and 2020, the Black male vote doubled, and even the Asian vote grew. While racism clearly played the largest role in motivating swing voters toward the Trumpist Republican faction in 2016 and continues to be an effective dog whistle, voting shifts in 2020 clarify that other factors are also driving the social support for authoritarian policies.

For White, working-class men and women, for example, suicide, opioid addiction, and alcoholism have lowered life expectancies—an unprecedented fate for a developed country. Men of all races without college degrees also face low marriage rates, high births out of wedlock, and declining social capital, all of which leave them lonelier. Women will soon out-graduate men from college two to one. America now has a large reservoir of men under 30—the most violence-prone group in any society—who have low levels of education, lack marriage possibilities and access to steady and well-paying jobs, feel humiliated by their low status in a country where downward mobility is seen as personal failure and in a working class culture where they expect themselves to be providers, and who must also hear high-status individuals tell them how privileged they are because of their gender and possibly race.

Anger at having these more complex cultural, economic, and identity concerns dismissed by elites as racism is being harnessed and weaponized by adversaries of democracy. Feelings of disrespect are being cultivated by an antidemocratic faction to drive together a large contingent of the country. Decades of studies of international insurgencies suggest that answering the legitimate grievances of groups, particularly concerns about corruption or unfairness, is important for diffusing conflict. How can the pro-democracy community stop unwittingly fusing these groups together and instead untangle this skein by understanding and answering the grievances that can be legitimately addressed?

Of course, working-class White people continue to hold privilege over working-class people of color historically and currently in hiring, housing, and many other spheres. But the knowledge that someone else has it worse does not erase a sense of resentment when one's life is tough enough and people with vastly greater wealth and power deride its difficulty. There are also real costs to a strategy of competitive victimhood, rather than a politics of inclusivity. Jardina has found that white identity politics emerge periodically in times where the White population feels under threat, such as the current demographic moment. But even in such eras, the 30 to 40 percent of White people who feel a growing sense of white identity can avoid accompanying that feeling with racial hostility—if fears of threat are calmed. There are many ways to calm such fears—such as unionization, which elevates the role of class in one's identity, or more inclusive rhetoric that ties issues of class and race together. Instead, unfortunately, it is not just the right that is increasing the sense of threat. Left-wing tropes about the coming majority-minority country and simplistic concepts of racial identity amplify White people's anxiety and ironically increase the likelihood that a white sense of identity will be accompanied by racism and actions against other groups, from voting contrary to minority interests to actual violence. For instance, researchers have found that priming White college students who identify strongly with their white identity to think about white privilege led them to express greater racial resentment.

Disarming the political weaponization of masculinity, race, religion, and class requires efforts that:

Reduce extremism within particularly at-risk populations such as evangelicals, veterans, and discrete right-wing communities supportive of violence by supporting organizations already trusted by these populations to reduce chances for extremist recruitment, build moderate voices, and create social groups supportive of speaking in favor of democracy and against violence.

Invest in a positive vision of masculinity and masculine citizenship. The movement to offer more positive views of women's and girls' roles in society has been of immense importance to altering social norms over the last fifty years. Yet it has not been accompanied by mass efforts to craft a mainstream, positive view of masculinity to stand alongside these empowered women and girls. On the right, efforts to create a positive masculine vision have curdled toward reinforcing male dominance. Among progressives, understanding of the concept of "toxic masculinity" is strong, but a positive vision that holds space for emotionally and socially healthy men who also like pickup trucks, hunting, physical labor, physical strength, and traditionally masculine pursuits is not. And neither vision is clear on where nonbinary individuals fit into their views on gender.

This need for a new masculine frame that affirms a positive vision of masculinity is also important because of the interlinked nature of white male citizenship and guns in America today. Political scientist Alexandra Filindra found that, in 2015, 43 percent of White men viewed owning a gun as a sign of good citizenship, a view particularly strong among White male gun owners who score high on surveys of anti-Black prejudice. These views have deep roots: laws since the nation's founding have conflated White men bearing arms with community protection. In the early days of America's colonies, and again after the Civil War, some states legislated that White men were required to bear arms, while Black men were barred from doing so. While gun ownership can certainly coincide with being pro democracy in the twenty-first century, that confluence requires notions of masculinity that encourage self-control—something the United States has actively supported in programming in places like Afghanistan. In the current moment of heightened political violence, finding ways to differentiate White male citizenship from so-called community protection would reduce the traction that militias such as the Oathkeepers and Three Percenters have gained. These militias depend on the notion that armed protest and vigilante community protection are acts of citizenship similar to voting.

Like all human beings, men need to feel that they hold roles that are valued in society, not in spite of but because of who they are. They cannot simply be admonished to refrain from negative actions—they require a positive and aspirational view of manhood that enables their full selves rather than requiring them to stifle parts of their identities. For instance, values that support democracy, such as honor, responsibility, hard work, and sacrifice, are among the virtues associated with masculinity by traditionalists.

For a healthy twenty-first-century society, these roles must support empowered women and nonbinary individuals, not come at their expense. Similarly, men must perceive that empowering women and nonbinary individuals also supports individual men's well-being, not that the groups are in competition for the top of a hierarchy. Programs intended to build such mutual regard are regularly incorporated into work in developing nations such as India, where some microcredit programs for women, for instance, also work with men to show them how wives who can read and save money actually support their families and their husbands' social ranks rather than undermine poor men's fragile grip on status.

There is a nascent effort to create healthy visions of masculinity in the United States. It includes ad campaigns for mainstream male products, nonprofits that focus on sports and other pursuits while bringing in more attuned ideas of manhood, and school programs that teach emotional intelligence and regulation skills to students of all genders. America needs more programs like these, as well as programs that offer healthy visions of mutually supportive and empowered genders within evangelical Christianity, where a negative version of masculinity has taken hold in recent decades.

Rethink how economic structures could better support democracy. Though class and inequality are components of America's social divisions, government-led economic redistribution won't address the problems of democracy. Government redistribution programs actually increase the threats to masculinity by deepening a sense of dependence. Reforms that are means-tested are particularly disliked by working- and middle-class Americans, who are more motivated by the fear of losing what they have to higher taxes than by the prospect of gaining more. Their disgruntlement is enhanced when programs are targeted at those who have even less, pitting the working class against those who are not working. Finally, years of dog-whistle politics have succeeded in inaccurately relating means-tested redistribution programs with African Americans, meaning that government redistribution measures intended to reduce inequality and poverty tend to increase racism. America can take a page from the international development field, which has spent twenty years learning that government-provided services intended to enhance government legitimacy can backfire because of the inevitable jealousies and misinformation that arise over who gets what, when.

Despite these problems with simple redistribution to ameliorate class grievances, the long-term loss of well-paying (and often male) manufacturing and other laboring jobs is playing a deep role in disempowering people who want to draw dignity from work and, instead, pushing them to look to more polarizing identity markers such as race for status.

American democracy does not need a simplistic redistribution that, however well-intentioned, backfires, but it does need a deeper rethinking of how economic structures could better support democracy and a holistic approach to how to alter them—the sort of work the Hewlett Foundation is supporting. Democratic scholars since Aristotle have noted that a broad middle class is crucial to democracy, while a resentful class facing loss is a major risk, acute poverty can be co-opted by politicians offering handouts, and oligarchic concentrations of wealth skew voters, policy, and politicians. The pro democracy community would do well to revive an old strain of democratic thought that also grounded the thinking of some of the country's founders, who believed that policymakers must consider how economic structures help or harm democracy—from concentrations of wealth to forms of work that remove the habits of free choice or association.

Return social status and higher wages to laboring jobs that don't require a college education. The Great Resignation and the low unemployment rate offer an opportunity to return better pay and, just as important, respect, to jobs that require manual labor but not college degrees.

Nearly two-thirds of American men don't have a college degree. And today, they are significantly less likely than women to complete high school, to enroll in college, and to graduate college. Society's respect for working-class labor therefore affects most men. It is also possible that conservative, white-collar men view attitudes toward traditionally male laboring jobs as proxies for society's respect for traditional male status.

The lower status of non-college-degree-requiring jobs also plays into hostile sexism. Starting with the generation born in 1974, women have consistently outpaced men educationally. Many White men seem to have made a personal choice not to compete with women—about four in ten claim they "just don't want to" continue schooling, transforming an aspirational norm of universal college education into a source of resentment. That means that rhetoric matters as much as programming. For instance, former president Barack Obama vastly increased the nation's apprenticeship programs, and Trump increased them as well—but Obama also vocally emphasized college as a goal that everyone should reach for, undermining the status his programs could have given to these skilled-labor jobs. How well a job pays and how much attention it receives from government leaders can serve as indicators of status if consciously deployed to serve that function. Political leaders should be encouraged to support apprenticeships, short-term training, certifications, and other skilled labor programs, as well as considering programs such as community-college-with-training efforts. The Chamber of Commerce and local business communities could support privately funded but similar programs, as well as deploy supportive rhetoric. In some fields, reducing credentialing requirements might be useful for cutting barriers to entry. In others, gradients of credentialing might provide greater status and income to skilled laborers, so long as these barriers are not used to exclude minority groups. These are empirical questions that require studying by industry.

Unions can also help bring greater recognition and financial compensation to these roles. Unionization also appears to have the positive effect of reducing racism, possibly by emphasizing class solidarity over racial difference: studies have found that gaining union membership between 2010 and 2016 reduced racial resentment among White workers.

Revitalize rural America. The decline of rural America is leaving the rural working class in an economic riptide, constantly pulling their stability out from under them. A problem rooted in economics has spread to opioid addiction and violence: the murder rate that has risen nationwide since 2020 also rose sharply in rural America, particularly in red states. The geographic concentration of violence means that in urban areas, the 30 percent rise in murders the United States experienced largely affects people living in a few very hard hit blocks. In a rural area, the same rate of increase is felt across a community because there are so many fewer people. Yet working-class Americans, who make up a greater percentage of rural America, are less likely to move due to the value they place on family, geographic roots, and economic needs that encourage them to remain near family homes and support systems. Neither party has addressed this problem well, but antidemocratic forces are succeeding in framing the enemies as immigrants, Jews, people of color, and coastal elites who look down on the hard work, values, and needs of so-called flyover country. While both the working class and White demographics moved away from Trump in 2020 compared to 2016, rural voters increased their support for the Trumpist Republican faction. Because the Senate and electoral college give particular power to rural voters, these lived realities combined with adept framing are having immense electoral consequences.

Removing or seriously addressing the following grievances might help. The needed efforts are partially economic. But they are also about ensuring that regulations are appropriate to rural areas, where life is quite different from city life. They are also about returning agency to rural areas, where the ability to control one's destiny is of particular personal value and yet has been denuded due to economic forces, educational failures, and government regulations. Economic, social, and cultural efforts to revive rural America are unlikely to affect partisan voting—but they may be important to reducing the sense of grievance of being left behind that is fueling an extremist, authoritarian faction within a party.

Change the information space by fighting disinformation, misinformation, and malinformation and by rebuilding local media. Realities regarding status loss and who or what is to blame are seen through the prism of perceptions, not facts. Those perceptions are strongly shaped by the media. Much has been made of social media's pernicious effects on democracy. Its algorithms and business models exacerbate outrage and anger.

They also help recruit and provide platforms to extremists.

But in Europe, social media has not been found to have the polarizing effects that it has in the United States—some studies show that it can actually help bridge divides in highly polarized countries. A cross-country study on affective polarization finds that in the United States, the phenomenon predates the internet and correlates more closely with the rise of cable news. Surveys also find extremely negative democratic effects from far-right and right-wing television and radio such as Newsmax, One America News, and Fox, rather than social media. That finding is corroborated by studies of those who attended the January 6 rally. Only one-tenth of arrested insurrectionists received most of their news from social media; most favored conservative television and radio.

In other words: the broader media environment determines the ways that social media affects a population. Together, right-wing radio, television, and social media form an echo chamber in which traditional conservative media is as serious a problem as social media. Both traditional and social media must be addressed to affect disinformation, misinformation, and malinformation. Meanwhile, a strong local news environment and the existence of trusted media of record can reduce polarization and help democracy even without changes to social media.

Programming for solutions in the social media realm should consider three audiences who are affected differently by social media. The largest is a general audience who engages almost entirely with entertainment and social news. This population rarely chooses to consume political news on purpose. Since they, like most people, have homogenous groups of friends offline, social media's weak links to old acquaintances often helps them become more open-minded and less polarized.

Next, a small, highly partisan audience is becoming more entrenched in its views thanks to social media. For them, social media is highly polarizing. Most of their feeds reinforce the rightness of their views, while the occasional opposing viewpoints from former friends or family polarizes them further. More media-sophisticated partisans are more susceptible to sharing misinformation and are more resistant to correction. This problem is occurring on the left and right; more educated, media-consuming liberals tend to have the most distorted views of the other party, while affective hatred and sharing of misinformation may be slightly greater among Republicans, possibly because they are older or because of the deeper echo chamber of both online and offline media on the right. Because highly educated partisans are the social group that is closest to most pro-democracy activists, these polarizing effects of the media tend to resonate with the pro democracy world and these groups' experiences are often seen as the whole landscape.

The third audience is the smallest but the most dangerous. It consists of individuals who seek out more specialized platforms such as 4chan, 8kun, Gab, and closed groups on Facebook, Telegram, and other sites in which to revel in hateful memes and jokes. This same small group also interacts differently with mainstream social media: studies of YouTube show that most engagement with extremist content on that platform was largely confined to a small, concentrated group of people who had preexisting negative views on gender and race. The amount of hateful discussion in these online fora is predictive of offline action. People who frequent hate sites are densely connected, seem to be mobilized to retweet more frequently, and are coordinated for attack.

These online populations follow a classic power law: a small number of people are responsible for a great deal of the online problem.

Actions to mitigate the dangers of social media should take these different audiences into account, focusing most action on the third group and undertaking careful, empirically tested work on the second. For the first group, simply providing easy access to good information is often enough. Efforts should aim to:

Rebuild local news sources . Trusted local media appears to serve as a bulwark against rabbit holes, democracy-eroding corruption, and polarization. Local media is also correlated with a host of prodemocratic habits from voting and split-ticket voting to civic participation. Local media appears to amplify the effects of countermeasures that help fight disinformation, misinformation, and malinformation. Its eclipse in recent years has opened space for more polarized news. Supporting many efforts underway to reinvigorate local journalism and provide local news sources to communities helps break polarization and democratic decline.

Launch mass campaigns using positive messaging to meet people's information needs' information needs and inoculation techniques to fight extremism . Inoculation techniques and efforts as simple as suggesting that people look up from their computers and connect with their families have been shown to de-escalate violence and stop the spread of disinformation, even among deeply committed anti democrats. These must be driven by constant testing and can be employed to pull people away from disinformation, misinformation, and malinformation and toward more positive community and family associations.

A significant number of people find their way down rabbit holes into disinformation, misinformation, and malinformation because good information appears lower in algorithms and thus in search results—or because facts appear behind paywalls that block poorer and less-partisan individuals. Fox News is free; the Washington Post, the New York Times, and many local news sites are not. The democracy movement should invest in web-savvy campaigns and consultants as part and parcel of philanthropic giving to ensure that it is easy for people to find good information and avoid bad.

Advocate for social media platforms to deplatform high-profile individuals but only demote vitriolic but lower-profile accounts as deplatforming can exacerbate their extremism, for the gaming industry to promote efforts for self-policing, and for Congress to regulate the core business model of social media platforms that profit from outrage and polarization. These advocacy efforts are hard and slow-moving but could all help fight disinformation, misinformation, and malinformation. Carefully deploy impact litigation against echo chambers responsible for defamation and other antidemocratic activities that are also illegal, to deter media propagandizing.

ENGAGE THE LEFT IN DEFENDING DEMOCRACY BY MAKING IT DELIVER

Democrats are not overly concerned about the threat posed by a right-wing faction that seeks to undermine democracy through the use of government.That may be due in part to recent victories:Whether one's side has won or lost an election is a factor in trust in elections, as is elite perceptions of the voting process.As a result, Democrats actually had a high level of trust in the 2020 election, and only 35% of Democrats express concern regarding the theft of democracy.

Yet, the absence of alert on the left about the deficiency of a majority rule government may likewise be on the grounds that numerous on the left, especially minority citizens and unfortunate electors, continue to be approached to end up voting to save a majority rule government, dismissing the way that majority rules government continues to neglect to address their issues.If voting does not provide them with a tangible benefit to their lives, organizations that claim to represent minorities or the poor will be unable to mobilize their base around abstract concepts like democracy.

Americans cannot build a brighter future without addressing the long-term concerns of those who are so disillusioned with government that they do not see the democratic system as one that serves them, even though the acute threats to democracy are largely coming from the right.Groups that have long been excluded from the full benefits of democracy cannot be provided with status and reassurance at the expense of groups that are traditionally higher up the social and political hierarchy.

According to high-quality studies of Black and Latino communities, these groups' policy goals center on improving the economy (fighting inflation, supporting higher-paying jobs, affordable housing, high-quality and affordable healthcare, and access to college), reducing racism, improving the air and water quality in their immediate neighborhoods rather than broader issues related to climate change, improving public schools, and reducing crime and improving immigration reform—in roughly that order.Democracy and voting issues are at the bottom of the list.That could be due, in part, to the fact that significant swaths of voters believe that their vote is irrelevant because neither party is seen as advancing these specific requirements.Under fifty-year-olds have a particularly strong opinion of these views.The issue stems not only from failing to actually raise the bar but also from failing to communicate successes.When people are worried that their kids will be sent to school in trailers, that their babies will go hungry, that they won't be able to pay for health insurance, and that voting won't change anything, democracy cannot be rallied around them.Additionally, despite the fact that many members of racial and ethnic minorities in the middle and upper classes do not personally experience these acute needs, they may identify with others from their racial or ethnic communities.The following initiatives ought to be the focus of organizations in order to shift the tide. Democracies should be based on real social and economic needs, especially those of underserved communities.Organizations for democracy ought to be aware of the fact that democracy cannot exist in an abstract state; rather, it needs to be embodied in addressing actual requirements that have an effect on actual people and in localities that are closest to the voters.The various communities that make up the left are less likely to support democracy goals unless they see strong movement on issues that matter to them and believe that organizations that claim to stand for democracy are supporting that movement.Core organizations in the pro-democracy universe need to work harder to support these communities on real-world issues that matter to them across racial, class, and ideological lines.

Highlight the ways in which social and economic goals are not being met due, in part, to democratic failures.Democracies ought to be a part of the agendas of groups that are formed to advance economic and social justice.This has been done in practice, for example, by focusing on voter suppression in its most recent State of Black America analysis.Some organizations in Michigan have emphasized that the

Flint water crisis was primarily caused by unelected emergency managers taking over disproportionately Black municipalities and not responding to voters. Recognize that the above-mentioned programs for men and the working class to address status anxiety also apply to minority working class men and should be designed and framed to assist both groups.In the past, Democrats were the party of the working class;This economic focus has been diluted by its strong pillars of support among minorities and college educated individuals.Republicans have always included business elites and are now welcoming the working class. However, they do so by prioritizing shared cultural beliefs over issues of race and class.Working-class minorities' specific needs are being left off the political agendas of both parties as a result of these shifts. initiatives aimed at creating a positive image of masculinity;raise the status and pay of skilled workers;minority men and working-class minorities on the left and the white working class and men on the right will benefit from countering disinformation, misinformation, and malinformation, which disproportionately target Black and Latino users of the internet.The most important thing is to make sure that these programs don't have any explicit or unintentional structures that make it hard for these communities to participate.Ideal would be to structure programs to appeal to people of all races.However, in some instances, different outreach and content will be required:For instance, disinformation targets White men and minorities in distinct ways, necessitating specific programming.

Provide information that is tailored to the requirements of minority groups.The importance of having access to information in achieving one's objectives cannot be overlooked by government programs and organizations that promote democracy as well as social and economic justice.Too many democracy and social justice organizations are failing to effectively communicate what has been accomplished by politicians and organizations or offer effective means of agency, despite the fact that a significant portion of the left's democratic dissatisfaction revolves around actually delivering policies that improve equality of opportunity and reduce systemic bias.Because typical searches for information do not yield the results that they are looking for, a significant portion of the anti-democracy disinformation, misinformation, and malinformation that disproportionately targets minority communities reaches them.

Media paywalls, as previously mentioned, are a factor in some of this.People who don't usually look for political information anyway seem unlikely to pay for news.One more issue is made by not giving data to bunches in the ways and at the times that they use it.For instance, educated progressives' rapid adoption of the term "Latinx" overlooks the fact that only 3% of Hispanics use the term.Because of this discrepancy, when the majority of Latino Americans search for information online, they will find information that is specifically targeted to the search terms they use and will miss information from groups that use Latinx.Frequently, calculations direct migrants toward data from their nations of beginning, including Spanish-language destinations abroad that have been immersed with Russian disinformation.

To reach minority and working-class audiences, democracy programming requires greater web savvy and cost considerations;Because it is necessary to meet people where they are, funding is essential.

Together, address police brutality, reform of the criminal justice system, and community safety.For quite a long time, ideological groups have bombed poor and minority networks by resolving the issues of criminal viciousness and police ruthlessness independently.

When the police, some of the most visible state representatives, behave brutally or with bias, democratic trust suffers greatly.Unfair justice is one of the quickest ways to lose a government's legitimacy, but globally, a sense that the state exercises power impartially is one of the best ways to build trust in the government and in fellow citizens.

However, plans to address the issues of brutal and unequal policing must also take into account the fact that civilian-on-civilian homicide is by far and away the leading cause of death for Black men in their twenties, accounting for more deaths than any of the other five causes taken together.One of the most pressing but least talked about equity issues in the nation is the high concentration of homicides in urban areas, which disproportionately affect minorities. These deaths, coupled with the fact that fewer than half of all homicides in the United States are currently solved, make this one of the most pressing issues.

No one's actual needs for safety can be met by mobilizing against criminal violence while ignoring state violence or by shielding individuals from the state while leaving them vulnerable to street violence.Rising levels of criminal activity run the risk of derailing criminal justice reform.In order to assist communities that ought to be protected by the state and, all too frequently, are not receiving it, these issue sets need to be addressed together with empirical evidence.As a result, efforts to eradicate extremism in law enforcement must be pursued vigorously.But it needs to be done with the police whenever possible so that it can be done in conjunction with evidence-based work, like focusing on the few places where the most crime happens and the few people who do the most violent things, to lower the skyrocketing murder rate, which was the highest it had been in over a century in 2020.Arrangement sets may likewise lie outside customary contemplating wrongdoing, for example, investigating the job mental social treatment can play, a specific need in minority networks underserved by injury informmed treatment.

BUILD A BROAD-BASED, MULTI STRAND, PRO DEMOCRACY MOVEMENT AROUND A POSITIVE VISION CONCRETIZED IN LOCALLY ROOTED ACTION

More than half of all Americans believe that the nation's best days are over.Many people believe that the system is corrupt and unsalvageable.Currently, only a small group of White, middle- to upper-class individuals engage in serious, positive pro-democracy work and mostly talk to each other.However, international democracy-support research reveals this categorically:In polarized democracies, broad constituencies of unlikely allies are needed to elicit significant change.Positive messages and concrete actions seem to motivate people worldwide, as evidenced by international examples.Eschewing national messages and issues in favor of local change is the best way to maintain the system's trust and avoid partisan polarization in U.S. democracy.

Many years of global work to help a majority rule government have observed that wide based social developments are the way to upsetting tyrant frameworks and that their solidarity lies in numbers as well as in their broadness across energized isolates.The electoral components that enable responsible conservatives to vote for democracy continue to be so crucial because America maintains a democracy.However, Americans can learn from movements that have prevailed in the face of more authoritarian odds.

To build a pro-democracy movement that is united, ideological partisanship is not the only divide that needs to be overcome.

The business community, religious leaders, the media, the police, and the military are just a few of the support pillars that all government systems rely on to maintain legitimacy.Individuals with complex personal goals, identities, and requirements make up these pillars.More of these pillars must join the pro-democracy side and eschew active or, more often, passive support for antidemocratic activities for democratic movements to succeed.Getting important people and groups from different pillars to publicly stand for democracy shows mainstream society that they can also do so without fear of retaliation.Additionally, it is necessary for overcoming the polarization that permits authoritarianism to gain support from voters.

To build a pro-democracy movement that is united, ideological partisanship is not the only divide that needs to be overcome.Depending on race, class, or age, numerous indicators of America's democratic health diverge.For instance, trust is a general public's safe framework, and it empowers networks to join against dangers and meet up to take care of issues.Social trust, or the belief that others will adhere to widely accepted social norms and that everyone shares common values and expectations, is the foundation of political trust in institutions.

It is well known that over the past sixty years, trust in democratic institutions and fellow Americans has decreased, with a sharp acceleration over the last twenty years.What is less known is that confidence in government really reached as far down as possible under Obama, hitting only 5% and 6 percent for the purported quiet and boomer ages, separately.However, while it was at its lowest point for White Americans, who continue to make up the majority of the population, it was on the rise for Black Americans.It is concerning that

Black and White people's levels of trust in the government began to diverge at that time and have continued to diverge ever since. This suggests that policies and politicians who increase the trust of one group are decreasing the trust of another.Without bridging this racial divide, Americans cannot establish widespread trust.

In contrast, Generation Z has the lowest level of trust of any generation and is significantly less committed to democracy.They must be brought into the pro-democracy space through generation-specific efforts.This may require civics instruction that includes historical and international examples of what can be lost and positive examples of what can be accomplished through collective action.

Lastly, the widespread belief that the system as a whole is rigged in favor of elites is one of the few issues that unites Americans of all political parties.This "vertical polarization" receives less attention than the left-right polarization, but it is just as severe, has allowed populist politicians to gain ground, and causes democracy messaging to fail for audiences who believe that the so-called democracy is biased against them.

Therefore, a pro-democracy movement's unity must work across parties, racial, generational, and class-cultural divides, as well as key societal pillars like the military, businesses, and religious institutions.Additionally, it needs to address divisions within these groups.Many immigrants are both racial minorities and believe they can rise to the top of America through hard work and do not wish to solidify their identities as outsiders. However, many racial minorities are progressive in some areas and hold more traditional religious beliefs.

The democratic movement needs to be based on a positive vision of what the country could be like. Authoritarians rely on division. Their strategy is to use fear and anger to divide society so that different parts of it will support them or at least feel conflicted enough to stay passive.Even for discrete pro-democratic purposes, widening divisions aids authoritarianism.However, the majority of partisan messaging aimed at encouraging voters to vote only serves to exacerbate existing divisions.It is easier to mobilize with a negative vision, but it is not sufficient to sustain success, as demonstrated by U.S.-based efforts to combat disinformation, misinformation, and malinformation as well as international experience building broad-based movements.multiple movements ending with "Enough!"They have won battles against authoritarian governments all over the world in their names, but when they try to consolidate a new system without a positive, inclusive vision, they lose their democracies to backlash.Even when pro-democracy candidates and issues use negative or fear-based messaging to win, it deepens polarization and encourages backlash that enlarges the authoritarian advantage over time.Also, when they lose, they increment agnosticism and sadness.

A pro-democracy movement must be based on a positive vision of what the country could be like if everyone saw the future as a win-win situation for themselves and their children.Some of the solutions to the country's democratic problems require recognizing the intersections of complex identities and needs, just as the efforts mentioned in the previous two sections could assist African American men disillusioned with decades of systematic mistreatment and White, right-wing men inclined toward extremism.Images, philosophical and policy concepts, and actions must be used to bring these concepts and feelings to life.

Lastly, local methods of engagement assist individuals in gaining agency and remaining grounded in what is clearly real rather than what nationalized media portrays as taking place.Local democratic practices will be altered as a result of some of this engagement.However, pro-democracy work cannot be entirely political because it would limit itself to a select few of the population who are interested in politics.Through positive, apolitical group activities like sports, concerts, community service, and dance—all of which offer moments of collective emotion—Americans must be reminded of what it means to come together and how that feels.These are all ways to emotionally engage Americans who may not be interested in politics or are too polarized to participate in pro-democracy activities.

Building a Movement Create a movement that brings together unlikely partners.Right and left, minorities and law enforcement, evangelical Christians and nonreligious people, younger and older voters, businesses and unions, and minorities and law enforcement all need to be positive, active, or passive members of a broad-based, prodemocratic social movement in which members of all groups can see themselves participating.

Creating intraparty and intragroup solidarity for democracy requires as much effort as cross-group efforts to bring together unlikely allies without losing flanks.It is not acceptable to label a conservative pro-democracy movement as anticonservative;Core progressive objectives cannot be sacrificed by a liberal democracy movement.Together for democracy, liberals and conservatives cannot simply be at the center of their parties, come from one generation, or be of the same race.

On the left, more work is required to address those who are willing to tolerate violence against businesses, personal property, and law enforcement, whereas intraparty work already excludes violent individuals who have aligned themselves with the antidemocratic side on the right.According to research on broad-based movements, violence of any kind—even from aligned movements or flanks—must absolutely be avoided because it quickly turns mainstream sentiment against them and reduces their breadth.Engaging with groups that might otherwise use violence to achieve their goals requires careful planning.

Developing trust, forming intra- and cross-group coalitions for democracy, and eventually taking public action will frequently take time and go unnoticed;Trust develops over time and can be damaged by excessive public scrutiny early on.These conferences, meetings, strategy sessions, and other activities that build trust and coalitions are necessary despite the slow returns on investment.

Narrative, Vision, and Philosophy Construct a positive, forward-looking, and inclusive vision of America that places all Americans in their rightful place and takes precedence over divisive visions on the left and right.This is not just a suggestion for how to communicate—Americans must first envision and articulate a positive future for themselves as a nation before they can do so.

Because many Russians believe that nothing can be changed and that nihilism is the only reasonable response, Putin controls Russia. Tyranny requires the consent of those tyrannized.Because they demonstrate that there is a possibility of a better path, people like Volodymyr Zelenskyy, the president of Ukraine, pose such a threat to Putin's regime.Instead of tyranny, the United States is facing the futility of fighting its fellow Americans to a standstill.The pro-democracy community is unable to think beyond avoiding a stolen election in 2024, which is understandable.However significant that objective may be, it is not something to anticipate.Crime, inflation, and the fear of their children's future being below them demoralize many Americans;Additionally, they are unable to visualize what the American dream might entail for them.Polarization is getting worse as a result of recent decisions by the Supreme Court.Polarization and sclerosis cannot be overcome with a zero-sum, scarcity mindset.

All Americans must be able to envision themselves as potentially successful, at ease, with agency, and with a voice in the narrative, which must present a common, optimistic view of America.Identity cannot be ignored in a future vision:ladies, racial minorities, and other character gathers band since they know personality fortitude is fundamental to being heard in a world that remains normed to White, Christian men.However, it must center the plurality of identities that each person possesses rather than the narrow notions of static, divided identities that are currently popular on the extreme right and left.

Both the identity-focused far left and the identity-obsessed far right present a vision of a society based on a hierarchy of static, thin, and unchangeable identity markers in which some groups are on top and those who lack a privileged identity cannot aspire to greater status. However, while the identity-focused far left and far right proclaim inclusion, the identity-obsessed far right trumpets exclusion.What is different is merely how groups are positioned in relation to one another, as well as who is allowed to speak and who is silenced.Backlash is being fueled by this zero-sum model of identity, which empowers white nationalist identity movements and antidemocratic activities by requiring certain groups to lose status and lose agency.Meanwhile, fear of status loss is dividing the potential prodemocracy movement and pitting subgroups against one another rather than uniting the nation against a white supremacist vision of America. This is best explained by the Western States Center's executive director, Eric Ward, in an interview that I highly recommend:

I disagree with the current fad that attributes empowerment to minority communities.However, I also strongly oppose the growing trend among minority community leaders to view identity politics as their ultimate goal.It's not.People-centered movements for justice are supposed to be rebuilt through identity politics.People are deprived of the fullness of their humanity when [static] narratives that force them into a position where their only identity is white, male, female, Jewish, or Black are strengthened.It simply does not reflect our human nature.

We will never be able to build a large enough movement or a common identity to defeat white supremacy systems or an emerging white nationalist movement because we will be subjugated to the role of an ally.We will only serve to perpetuate inequality.These blunders make it easier for even more regressive people to broaden their attacks on civil rights and other people-centered movements.

People must be able to live their full identities in a future-focused vision of what America could be, bringing those contradictions and complexities into a modern America where no one is automatically denied status due to any part of their identity.What does an America resemble where this happens?In order to construct a united pro-democracy movement, answering that question necessitates engaging it directly within and across groups.

Additionally, it is essential to take into consideration the activities of the pro-democracy community that may conflict with the construction of this vision.Even if those images turn the traditional hierarchy on its head, organizations and philanthropists should speak up if the rhetoric and imagery that the groups they support support a hierarchical image of society with static, unchanging, thin identities.

Build a new vision by investing in numerous areas.Before it can be shared, a positive vision must be imagined and believed.Focus groups and strategic communication alone are not enough to accomplish this.The pro-democracy community is too focused on defending the democracy that exists, largely in its more abstract, institutional form, to think big, while Americans who are exhausted, enraged, and cut off from one another do not have the capacity to consider a better future.

Considering a future together may appear Pollyanna-like right now.However, the alternative to a future spent apart is one spent in some way.Even though some on the right call for secession and others on the left would be thrilled to see them go, such a course of action is not only impractical and could be fatal, but it also allows the same cultural and political issues to persist in the same locations under a different national name.There is basically no alternate way forward except for to make a joint future.The international community demands that nations integrate individuals who have murdered, stolen from, beaten, and tortured their fellow citizens into communities and villages following a conflict.Are Americans so small-minded and unimaginative that partisans are unable to envision ways to coexist with those whose disagreements are not yet as pronounced?

The dreams Americans should assemble ought not be about the reflection of a vote based system itself — they ought to be about what Americans expect from their regular routine in America.This lived experience in the future needs to be rooted in reality.It's possible that exercises in deliberative democracy could be used to talk about a variety of aspects of day-to-day life as well as major culture war issues in order to diffuse the latter with ideas that use practical thinking to break down hardened polarization and raise shared hopes for the lives of Americans in the future.Instead of looking back nostalgically at an America in which a portion of the population was prevented from competing or offering a vision that frightens the people who remain the majority of the voting public, how does the nation achieve collectively the American Dream of the future?That is a significant undertaking on its own.

Establish a unified philosophy and foundational concepts.Philosophical, policy, and intellectual efforts that offer depth must also be supported by a narrative of a future that crosses the chasms of partisan polarization and elite-non elite polarization.If the United States did not have a dominant, assumed, and normative identity, how would and should policies change?What would the economic system change to support an America with more opportunities for those without college degrees and in rural and urban areas?How can the philosophical principles of "freedom from" and "freedom for" be put into practice at the same time?What guiding principle support such a dream, what values are subverted, and how are these qualities grounded in the nation's initial guidelines, strict texts, and different spots Americans go for significance and moral absolutes?How could Americans do better while simultaneously meeting other public service needs? Are the current efforts to group and list subcommunities beneficial or detrimental to complex identities?What could help these ideas find their footing and how would they work to upend assumptions within racial, religious, or other interest communities that could provoke backlash?Think tanks, special editions of serious magazines, and public intellectuals provide the best answers to these questions.To answer these questions in conversation with one another within and across societal divides, they require conferences and core support.

Spread these ideas around.Advertising and other mass-media efforts, in addition to artistic, literary, and cultural endeavors, will be required for dissemination to instill a concrete, pictorial vision of what a more inclusive America with complex identities and greater individual agency looks like and can be.Advertisers could, for example, collaborate with pro-democracy groups and narrative specialists to see what ideas emerge from focus groups targeting a variety of demographics. They could also test what kinds of rhetoric and imagery can pique the public's interest and counter the current great replacement theory trope that pits one group of Americans against another.The Chamber of Commerce and other business organizations might think about supporting online campaigns and public service announcements that reinforce this complex, optimistic, and forward-looking vision of America in order to improve the country's stability.

Journalism should also be involved, supporting reporting and editing that makes narratives more complicated and makes it easier for the American public to see full people with complicated identities.

Local, Concise Action Concepts and images must be made real through actual experience.The progressive movement was successful in part because it had many different strands in which people could participate. These strands ranged from building playgrounds on the local level to prison reform, ranked choice voting, and antitrust activities, where Americans could act locally or nationally.Local associations were at the heart of even abstract politics' ability to achieve goals.Progressive strategies for building broad-based and active coalitions that connected democratic reforms to social engagement and local action merit replication from a methodological standpoint.

Bring local politics back to life.Problems that are not being solved and national narratives that hide complexities, exacerbate polarization, and prevent communities from addressing obvious needs frustrate Americans.Communities need to be involved in finding practical solutions to real problems, especially in areas that are experiencing significant social dislocation, rapidly shifting demographics, an economic downturn, or rapid economic growth and inequality.People can develop civic attitudes and habits through such engagement at the local level, where trust is still at its highest.If well-massaged and moderated, local engagement on local issues can help people exercise their problem-solving muscles.

One example of many issues that have been politicized into binary caricatures is the controversy over education and curriculum, with debates fueled by national organizations like Moms for Liberty that are backed by national funds and a national agenda.However, the intensity indicates a strong demand for solutions from both political parties.Many parents, who are being pushed to extremes or silenced, actually hold complex, mixed views, ranging from those who were disappointed by what they saw during Zoom classes to those who saw their children's educational attainment and mental health suffer during prolonged school closures.Engagements based on Democracy in One Room, which brought together hundreds of Americans in a representative sample to discuss difficult topics in a moderated setting with factual information provided throughout, may reduce shouting and provide parents with a means to improve their children's lives and comprehend the challenges faced by their schools and teachers.

These models of deliberative democracy might be able to connect with Americans in a variety of areas where they already have a lot of passion and help them come up with sensible solutions that break down cultural divides.Climate change is a national and polarized issue, just like education.But fires, floods, and tornadoes are increasingly affecting many communities, and they can work together to develop local resilience.People can practice problem-solving skills in real-world situations where they must deal with the complexities of other people's lives and desires, reducing the national stereotypes of other people.

From citizen assemblies (which in Ireland have been used to recommend constitutional and legislative referendums on issues ranging from abortion to the structure of Dublin's local government) to participatory budgeting (such as when Madrid allocated 100 million euros of its municipal budget through citizen rankings of projects in order of preference), localities can experiment with a variety of new democratic methods to increase engagement.The International Observatory on Participatory Democracy gathers examples of these methods in Europe for the United States to study.

bolster local social engagements that are wholesome and cohesive.Experience must be incorporated into the narrative.But social engagement has been declining for decades in the United States.A study of Weimar Germany revealed that Nazi membership grew more quickly in areas with a higher concentration of community organizations.There is a correlation between higher levels of belief in conspiracy theories and greater right-wing involvement in community groups and attendance at white evangelical churches in the United States.

Instead, it's important to engage in social activities that bring people together for common goals and bridge differences.However, many of the so-called "bridging programs" have serious flaws:They fail to reach their intended audiences because they self-select individuals who have the time and ideological preferences that make them open to such engagement.They frequently move toward a mealy middle that does not respect real differences or honor different identities.They also run the risk of reifying and hardening identities of partisanship or other differences by asking people to show up in those identities.Rather than engaging in constructive work, many people rely solely on conversation, which, according to research, is insufficient for success.Rather, what is required is:

Avoid bridging divides for the sake of bridging them; instead, embrace self-help for mutual benefit. Americans must work together despite their differences.However, self-conscious bridging programs exclude Americans who are more or less political.Organizations that provide them with some benefit are more likely to involve these key groups than those that are specifically focused on our nation's healing.In the past, unions provided skilled laborers, in particular, with cross-partisan social activities.The choice to spend time with a disparate group of people with whom one has little in common other than a job is unique to unions because it directly benefits the giver.People who are pressed for time or otherwise uninterested in cross-partisan or cross-racial engagement are more likely to be reached by civic commitments that include this kind of self-help.

The various twelve-step groups for alcoholics, drug addicts, and similar groups, which maintain that connection is the opposite of addiction, are some of the most prominent examples of such cross-partisan engagement for mutual benefit today. These groups are in addition to unions.Locally based meetings are intimate and intimately personal, with high levels of personal engagement where partisan identity is irrelevant and the shared identity of overcoming addiction unites people.Sadly, opioid use has now crossed racial and class lines, making these groups an important way for people of all backgrounds to meet and form communities in the United States.Imagine a scenario where piece of the association such gatherings cultivated was association with our urban texture, adding a positive feeling of organization and the strengthening of local area administration to the relational recuperating.

In other nations, lending circles are common. These groups of people meet on a regular basis to divide funds, take out loans, and assist one another with entrepreneurial endeavors. They are an updated version of the old mutual aid and burial associations.They are just getting started in the United States, where they can help the one-third of adult Americans with low credit scores or no credit history build credit, build community, and provide essential financial support.

There are numerous other forms of mutual self-help:With the provision of civic space, the organization of tournaments, and volunteer opportunities for trail construction, field enhancement, and other tangible outcomes, sports and recreation groups for adults or families could also be encouraged.What if the need to connect across differences and the desire to connect with the divine were combined? Religion is one of the most racially and politically divided areas in the nation.A tool lending library, occasional how-to classes sponsored by the city or private sector, civic space and encouragement, and mutual help groups for gardening, landscaping, and construction could be of assistance.Cities will actually reap greater civic benefits than if they overprovide for these endeavors by providing assistance but requiring volunteer time in return.

According to research, one of the best ways to change perceptions and polarization is to create a third identity through constructive engagement. This suggests that these programs should aim to bring people together from different social groups.However, these programs should not be presented in an overtly political or democratic manner in order to attract participation from the most disadvantaged individuals;The objective is to develop alternative forms of social problem-solving and community involvement that transcend partisan divides and instead unite people from different backgrounds. Invest in social activities that merely remind individuals that doing things together as a community is enjoyable.Civic festivals that require participation, like Mardi Gras in New Orleans, should be encouraged to be held by mayors. These festivals include community concerts, movies, clean-up days, family sports days, and civic festivals with low barriers to entry and time commitments that can range from minimal to substantial.

To build on the previous ideas, events that specifically target men should be front and center, like father-child sporting events, coaching opportunities, rebuilding the homes of the elderly, or activities like Habitat for Humanity that give men a chance to play roles that are respected and positive in their communities.Events of this nature are unlikely to significantly bridge partisan divides given the extent of geographic partisan sorting.Instead, they are attempts to assist individuals who are experiencing feelings of solitude, anomie, and personal dislocation in finding positive communities that connect them to American ideals rather than leaving them to form violent online associations.

Make use of social urbanism.To bridge class and racial divides, such events should, whenever possible, encourage mixing from various municipalities.For instance, popular city concerts were held in low-income areas of Medellin, Colombia, in an effort to combat violence and foster a common civic identity.Additionally, in order to reshape the civic fabric, desirable civic infrastructure, such as an internationally renowned architect's library, was constructed in less desirable areas of the town.

These "social urbanism" ideas should be considered by the United States in order to use urban planning to benefit democracy.After all, thinkers like Thomas Jefferson, a former president, and Alexis de Tocqueville, a French historian, recognized the significance of town squares in New England as a symbol of the country's emerging democracy.What would a place geography look like if it supported democracy and removed obstacles posed by inequality at its current levels?Universities and conferences on urban planning might be good places to start with this question.

Develop strategies for community and municipal resilience.Whitefish, Montana, and other communities have used replicable strategies to combat hate and unite their communities.Nonprofits, the DOJ's Community Relations Service, and the Federal Mediation and Conciliation Service should be supported in their efforts to collaborate with state and municipal officials to develop early warning and response systems that bring together diverse groups—such as religious organizations, businesses, trusted local media, local government, and other stakeholders—to quell rumors and deal with threats in specific localities or communities where tensions are high or where data or trends indicate the likelihood of greater tension.The DOJ's Community Relations Service should receive more funding so that it can expand its role in training communities and law enforcement in ways to prevent and respond to hate-fueled violence, address hate crimes, and develop ongoing, sustainable community-based methods. Nonprofits with mediation experience can also help expand its reach.

STRENGTHEN ACCOUNTABILITY TO RESET NORMS ON WHAT BEHAVIOR IS LEGAL AND ACCEPTABLE

A strategy to support democracy requires sticks as well as carrots. There are red lines that must be upheld for democracy to work. Those who lose elections have to accept defeat. Those who interfere in elections must be denounced and brought to account. Violence can have no place in democratic life. Corruption poisons trust—

whether corrupt actions are technically legal or not. Politicians and wealthy elites cannot be above the laws that bind the rest of the people.

it is crucial to have a united and cross-party democracy movement of unlikely allies to engage in and support accountability together.

Accountability from the state and from society matters in determining what is viewed as acceptable political and social behavior and what is unthinkable. The more laws must be brought to bear, the more the rule of law will be strained—for that reason, wherever possible, it is better to assert social norms to curb antidemocratic behavior. However, as these social norms give way, the legal net below is too threadbare to catch the free fall of U.S. democracy. It needs shoring up.

Accountability must be carefully deployed to avoid backlash. In other countries, when state actions to quell violent uprisings like the militia movement in the United States castanet broad enough to include innocents or involve state violence in return, the result is the growth of the very movements that governments are trying to squelch. Because the actions below to hold people to account can be falsely construed as antidemocratic by the fraction of Americans who believe that their efforts to counter election fraud and authoritarian pandemic mandates are fighting for democracy, it is crucial to have a united and cross-party democracy movement of unlikely allies to engage in and support accountability together. The more cross-ideological pillars of support to back these norms, the harder they will be to dismiss as partisan.

Reform the Electoral Count Act . This law from the post–Civil War period determines the final decision regarding national elections, and it is full of dangerous loopholes. As former federal circuit judge J. Michael Luttig articulated during the Select Committee on January 6 hearings, it needs rapid reform to clarify procedures in order to avoid democratic disaster in the case of a close election in 2024. Reform of the Electoral Count Act must be prioritized even if a broader set of desirable reforms turn out to be impossible.

Use civil impact litigation to try to bankrupt and deter violent and extreme antidemocratic groups. This strategy has been used against the Unite the Right and January 6 rally organizers; individuals who have engaged in intimidation and violence, like the founder of the neo-Nazi website Daily Stormer; and media organizations such as the Gateway Pundit and One America News Network that appear to assist in the spread of violence and disinformation.

Pursue criminal lawsuits against individuals who undertake violence, threaten officials, or break democratic laws. While criminal law is the purview of the government, outside organizations can help states understand and use lesser-known laws, and philanthropy can assist these groups.

Bring lawsuits against government bodies to force them to uphold equality under the law, protect rights, and avoid misuse of government services. These lawsuits are particularly important to bring against law enforcement bodies to convince voters that laws will be applied equally and will protect all. For example, there

are important lawsuits against the Department of
Homeland Security following its federal deployment of
riot police in Portland and against local Texas police
who refused to assist calls for help as a Biden campaign
convoy was attacked by pro-Trump drivers.
Ensure professional accountability , such as being
disbarred, for lawyers who violate democratic norms.
Other professional norm-setting bodies and entities
should be used to hold members accountable and
uphold democratic norms.
Bring legal challenges and support legal scholars
to build and advance long-term legal theories that
enhance prodemocratic norms. Some of this work will
be defensive, such as undermining efforts to enshrine
the independent state legislature theory that is being
revived despite the significant violence it enabled
around elections throughout the nineteenth century.
Other aspects must be forward-looking, to build the legal
foundation for an economy of greater opportunity, for
example, or to ground group and individual rights in a
manner that enables greater identity complexity.
Clarify state and federal laws and doctrine against
violence to make them easier to adjudicate or to enable
greater deterrence. Measures could include:
extending protections against intimidation from election
officials to immediate family members, contractors, and
vendors;
extending the doctrine to strengthen the rules against
extremism within the active-duty military to the laws that
govern federal law enforcement, particularly at the

Department of Homeland Security and the Department of Justice; and

clarifying legal conditions and precedent to remove extremists in local law enforcement.

Increase accountability for political elites and white-collar criminals. The sense that the wealthy are buying American politics is widespread and corrosive to trust in democracy—both Biden and Trump voters listed accountability for public leaders as their fifth most important value in an in-depth survey.

Often these concerns are translated into efforts to curb money in politics. Such work is currently doomed, given the composition of the Supreme Court and precedents on money equaling speech. Moreover, efforts to limit campaign spending can backfire: plutocratic money will always find a way to affect the system when big issues that affect businesses or wealthy ideologues are on the table. Meanwhile, small-dollar donors are not necessarily better for democracy: small-dollar donations tend to support anti establishment candidates, which means they also support more polarizing candidates on the left and right. Small-dollar donations surged after January 6 when some corporations temporarily cut funding to candidates who supported the insurrection. The most extreme Republican candidates, such as Greene, bought expensive fundraising lists and used them to fundraise from small-dollar donors while building an image of widespread grassroots appeal. Meanwhile, limiting donation amounts leads candidates to waste inordinate time on fundraising, forcing them to spend more time with wealthy givers. Their lack of time leads them to lean even more on lobbyists for policy information, allowing money to influence policy through even more direct routes than donations.

Thus, a more orthogonal approach focused on accountability for the wealthy and well-connected instead of on campaign donations may achieve more while meeting the actual desires of more Americans for accountability of elites. Although overt corruption in America is quite low, the sense that the system is rigged is in part based on legal activities that feel unfair to many Americans—such as the ability of corporations and wealthy individuals to avoid taxes. It has not been lost on the American public that financial elites impoverished millions in 2008, with few repercussions, or that much of the campaign support that is legally allowed in America feels corrupt. Nearly three-quarters of Americans are somewhat or very dissatisfied with the influence of major corporations on democracy (though, crucially, nearly the same amount trust small business). Increasing taxes for the extremely wealthy, closing loopholes for them and for corporations, and other activities that make people believe that plutocrats are paying their share and abiding by the same laws are crucial for enhancing the public's belief in the democratic system.

One step is shining light on the problem—but internationally, transparency without change can actually enhance the public's view that their political system is rigged. Therefore, efforts to reduce corruption and legal activities that appear to benefit political and financial elites must not only shine light but also enhance actual accountability and repercussions. This has been made harder by the Supreme Court, but the issue is not as intractable as campaign finance reform is.

Pursue Supreme Court term limits. While courts still enjoy higher levels of trust than U.S. politicians and electoral institutions, the overturning of Roe v. Wade after multiple justices declared the case as settled precedent in front of Congress feels to many on the left like perjury before Congress, which is itself a crime. The lack of ethics rules also undermines trust. Recent court decisions also enable political corruption, further undermining faith in the democratic system.

Until the 1960s, the average tenure of a supreme court justice was fifteen years; it is now twenty-six years. Majorities of both parties support limiting the tenure of Supreme Court justices—in May 2022, term limits garnered 60 percent support—even as they disagree about adding justices to the court's number. There is historical precedent in which to ground a change to tenure and service. At the country's founding, Supreme Court judges "rode circuit," which meant serving simultaneously as Supreme Court and lower federal court judges. These roles were only separated in the 1800s by an act of Congress, not a constitutional amendment. Biden's Presidential Commission on the Supreme Court of the United States has a long discourse regarding the possibility of returning to such an arrangement based on federal judges serving eighteen-year-long Supreme Court stints with term limits, which would allow each president to choose an equal number of justices each term. While such a change would be seen as political in the current moment, it might assist in depoliticizing court confirmations and lowering the stakes over the long term. Meanwhile, ethics rules for the Supreme Court are wise and extremely popular.

COMMON STRATEGIES THAT ARE INSUFFICIENT TO ALTER THE TRAJECTORY OF U.S. DEMOCRACY

American democracy is starting to drown.

Philanthropists are investing in a number of strategies that are treading water. These are essential for keeping democracy alive and important to invest in. But they are not able to get the country out of the current situation.

In preparation for the 2024 elections, some philanthropists are crafting a multi-hundred-million-dollar effort to protect the election. A similar effort in 2020 funded crucial activities that contributed to a free and fair election and potentially prevented an even more precipitous democratic decline that could have been predicted from a second Trump term. Without those efforts, democracy would be in a far worse place today. However, despite significant funds, such activities did not alter the negative trajectory of U.S. democracy. If anything, democratic decline has sped up at the state level. Because these strategies are major planks of pro-democracy activity and philanthropy, it is worth spelling out why they are necessary but insufficient to meet the challenge. For the foreseeable future, U.S. democracy will need a both-and, not an either-or, solution set.

Help Democrats win. A number of the theories below may be executed as good faith, nonpartisan strategies or may be pursued subconsciously or more explicitly to help Democrats win until the Republican Party becomes a prodemocratic party again. Given the revelations surrounding Trump's efforts to overturn a legitimate election in 2020, and the fact that many who aided his efforts on Capitol Hill and in some states are still in power, these strategies are important to forestalling more rapid democratic decline, especially if Trump runs in 2024.

However, a strategy grounded in helping Democrats win to save democracy is 100 percent certain to fail. In twenty states, Republicans already hold both legislative chambers and the roles of governor, attorney general, and secretary of state. Democrats cannot realistically alter state policies in these states through government control; they must change minds. Nationally, the constitutional framework—combined with strong national support for Republicans and the redistricting of seats in the House of Representatives that just occurred following the 2020 census and will last for the next decade—means that the Republican Party is very likely to win power over Congress and/or the presidency before it ends its current antidemocratic tactics. And perhaps most problematic for this strategy is experience: after 2020, Democrats won control of the presidency and both chambers of Congress—and democratic degradation nevertheless advanced rapidly at the state level and within society.

Meanwhile, the perception of partisan bias in pro democracy activities may be sharpening divisions and precluding efforts to bolster democracy.

Increase voter turnout. More Americans voted in 2020 than in any modern election. Both parties experienced significant gains. Meanwhile, the number of antidemocratic election law alterations at the state level grew, as did increases in violent threats, while trust in elections eroded greatly among Republicans and Independents.

Get more minorities to vote. This strategy often tries to marry the fact that challenges to voting disproportionately target minorities and that people of color have historically voted Democratic. However, by attempting to kill two birds with one stone, it risks missing both.

Targeting all the laws being passed to suppress voting fails to prioritize those that most harm both minorities and democracy. For instance, no state had voter identification requirements before 2006, making them a long-term focus of the democracy community hoping to help minority voters. While voter identification laws don't have overall effects on turnout, some studies suggest that they do suppress minority votes, particularly of Latinos. Other large, credible studies find no negative effect on any demographic group (nor any effect on fraud). Meanwhile, voter identification laws are supported by large majorities of Black voters (66 percent), Hispanic voters (77 percent), and Asian voters (75 percent), meaning that fighting battles to remove identification requirements yields equivocal outcomes that aren't supported by the communities that activists are purporting to help.

Similarly, I love mail-in voting and personally wrote in its support in multiple venues in 2020 because of its importance to an election held during a pandemic prior to vaccine availability. Mail-in ballots accounted for nearly half the 2020 ballots. But its use was miniscule before 2000—when U.S. democracy was in better shape. It largely expanded, for good reason, because of fears of large gatherings during a deadly, contagious pandemic. Meanwhile, there's no evidence behind claims that it benefits Democrats, and its record with improving minority turnout is mixed. (Though theoretically helpful for preventing problems with long election lines, fears of violence, or an inability to get time off from work on election day, African Americans tend to use it less, in part due to justified fears that their ballots will be disproportionately disqualified, while Hispanic or elderly voters use it the most).

Linking important voting measures that have public support with those that don't opens the entire agenda to questioning. To maintain credibility and focus, pro-democracy efforts to help minorities vote should target the rules that are empirically proven to have harmful effects such as longer wait times, caused in part by reduced Sunday voting and reduced voting locations. Ideally, they would target those that both have harmful effects and are felt by minority voters themselves to be most problematic.

For those pursuing minority votes in the hopes of increasing Democratic chances, the realities in crucial states such as Florida—which now comprises over a tenth of the votes for the electoral college—are becoming more mixed. Racial minorities have multiple identities: they may also be male, religious, working class, rural, or immigrants from communist nations, allowing their votes to be harnessed by politicians who can speak to other elements of their identities that may be more salient to them. Latino voters have never been a monolith. They showed more conservative voting patterns in the 2020 election than in 2016, and majorities of second-generation immigrants saw themselves as "typical Americans" in a reply to a survey question with that wording. Majorities of immigrants are more concerned with economic than social issues. And nearly ten percent of Black Americans are now immigrants, which is one potential reason for the increase in Black male votes for Trump—which reached nearly a third in high-immigration states like Minnesota. Among those who are immigrants from former communist countries, many have been targeted by disinformation, misinformation, and malinformation and are proponents of the "big lie," which implies that Trump actually won the 2020 election. Moreover, negative partisanship means that identity-based campaigns may increase turnout for the other side.

Court more swing voters. The alternative to a base-vote theory is a swing-voter theory. This is difficult, but not impossible, for moving voters away from Trump and other proponents of the big lie. The effort to court swing voters in partisan general elections through persuasion (as opposed to fielding a candidate who simply attracts this group) appears to rarely work without a strong ground game and other innovative tactics: there are just too few persuadable voters left, except in unusual races or with particularly careful targeting efforts. Persuadable voters do seem to move if they have been properly identified through experiments and then targeted with methods like real, face-to-face conversations. These efforts are worth engaging in for targeted races where they can make a difference. But very little of the money spent on persuasion actually goes to efforts shown to work: the vast majority is spent on advertising that has virtually no effect.

Meanwhile, for those wanting to move the country in a democratic direction rather than just voting for Democrats, there is another problem: the two groups of voters who are least likely to support democracy—those who have previously voted for different parties and those who do not vote consistently—also represent two key characteristics of swing voters. Swing voters show the strongest support for a third party—but not the one that many good-government types imagine. Only 4 percent of U.S. voters want a moderate party that is socially liberal and economically conservative. Instead, many support liberal economic redistribution combined with conservative cultural policies: they favor government help for themselves and others they deem "deserving" (a category with a strong racial tilt), combined with greater salience of a white, Christian, native-born identity, leaving them with a foot in both parties. Swing-voting White Americans—many of whom moved into the Republican Party in 2016—scored particularly high on racial resentment. Among these economic liberals and cultural conservatives,

Democracy Fund's Voter Study Group found that 52 percent supported a "strong leader" who need not bother with Congress or elections, and 40 percent did not favor democracy.

Neither a sense of being left behind economically nor changes to individual economic standing are correlated with Trump voters. These findings echo multiple other studies of terrorism, right-wing violence, and the January 6 insurrectionists that find that poverty, the decline of manufacturing, unemployment, and other economic factors are not predictive of right-wing violence in the United States.

Improve the electoral system. U.S. elections have real security challenges, such as software so outdated that software providers have declared that they will discontinue patches before 2024, as well as problems born of normal human errors that provide ready fodder for disinformation and distrust. Rebuilding faith in the electoral system must include bipartisan, compromise measures that make voting more secure and more accessible, such as those passed in Kentucky in 2021. It also requires efforts to simply improve local election administration, such as the U.S. Alliance for Election Excellence is doing. These efforts are important and necessary—fighting alleged fraud that did not occur is hard enough; arguing for democracy in the face of actually compromised elections would be far more difficult and is a reality that the country would have faced in 2020 but for a massive infusion of private capital to allow counties to purchase protective gear, pay workers, and otherwise run the 2020 elections.

Yet, technical reforms are not enough to alter the perceptions that are deliberately being seeded to undermine faith in elections. Colorado, for instance, has some of the nation's most technically proficient elections, as well as a virulent Stop the Steal movement. Facts don't alter beliefs. Meanwhile, the grants made in 2020 to make elections more secure actually fueled doubts in some people. Philanthropists hoping to use technical reform to actually strengthen election security are sensible. Those seeking to use such donations to strengthen belief in elections should look to the field of international development, where decades of research into using funding to strengthen government services in order to deepen government legitimacy show that such programs often enhance distrust, in part because they are inevitably delivered earlier or in greater amounts to some communities that are themselves distrusted. Increase economic redistribution. The acute degradation of U.S. democracy is not being caused by poverty, unemployment, or other causes of individual economic loss. Democracy Fund's Voter Study Group found no correlation between personal financial circumstances and support for authoritarianism. Neither a sense of being left behind economically nor changes to individual economic standing are correlated with Trump voters.. These findings echo multiple other studies of terrorism, right-wing violence, and the January 6 insurrectionists that find that poverty, the decline of manufacturing, unemployment, and other economic factors are not predictive of right-wing violence in the United States.

Those most frustrated with democracy are facing a sense of thwarted expectation based on the gap between what they are achieving and what they believe themselves to be entitled to. Data internationally shows that such perceptions are fairly impervious to rising individual incomes. In fact, in the United States, more economically developed states are most at risk of right-wing violence. Internationally, some research suggests that extremist politics may be most attractive to people who are doing less well than others within a growing economy (even if they are doing better than they had been doing previously), making economic redistribution a poor tool to target the problem.

Reforms to help individuals improve economically are useful—if directed toward disadvantaged minority communities, where concrete economic programs could address the democratic erosion caused by democracy's failure to deliver. But the victim narrative and grievance politics of the partisan right make doing so without backlash difficult, unless redistribution occurs across class lines. Meanwhile, for the reasons discussed earlier, economic redistribution programs will not address the drivers of democratic decline from the right. While government redistribution programs to individuals won't alleviate democratic challenges from the right, the economic structure of America is playing a role in enhancing status anxiety and allowing cultural issues that are stand-ins for class be weaponized for authoritarian ends. Economic shocks such as the 2008 recession do affect feelings toward the entire political system—particularly when the wealthy received bailouts and the working and middle classes did not. Inequality also enhances a sense of status loss and feelings that the system is rigged, as well as being highly correlated with violence. More work is needed in looking at what alterations to America's basic economic structure could help its democracy and what forms of implementation would work to concretize those goals.

Fix gerrymandering. The United States needs to have a serious conversation about gerrymandering. Allowing politicians to pick their constituents reduces trust in the system and enables the increase in safe seats that are driving extreme candidates.

Yet there are three problems with simply doing away with gerrymandering. First, it is easy to speak against partisan gerrymandering when the other side is doing it—but harder to defend unilateral disarmament. Second, racial gerrymandering is allowed under the Voting Rights Act, and it helps minority voters symbolically and substantively. Yet racial gerrymanders are seen as partisan by the right. Paradoxically, they may harm overall Democratic chances for gaining seats in the House of Representatives by packing large numbers into safe districts above what is required for representation. Moreover, because their votes matter disproportionately to one party, gerrymandering allows the other party to ignore, suppress, or even engage in violence against minority voters, a pattern that plays out around the world and that leads some other divided societies to undertake vote-pooling systems like ranked choice. Finally, voter-supported legislation to reduce gerrymandering—such as Florida's laws requiring districts to be built around contiguous areas—can undermine political and racial gerrymandering, leading to calls of racial unfairness. And, of course, much of the problem of safe seats has to do with voters self-sorting geographically, not gerrymandering itself.

Something that seems to voters so blatantly unfair must be addressed—and yet the solution set here is unclear. The United States needs new thinking, not doubling down on the old.

THREE POSSIBLE FUTURES

America is approaching three possible futures in the near term. These are not far-off prognostications. Instead, they are intended to hold a mirror to a future that is almost here, to show what is likely to solidify. Without significant, fast action, America could start to look like other:

stable countries run by one political party where voters cannot alter politics,

countries run by one political party whose control is upheld by violence, or

countries with political stalemates and increased criminal and political violence.

STABLE COUNTRIES RUN BY ONE POLITICAL PARTY WHERE VOTERS CANNOT ALTER POLITICS

Close elections in 2024 in states like Michigan, Pennsylvania, or Wisconsin lead local activists from the losing party to file allegations of fraud. Their goal is not to win, necessarily, but to delay certification and sow doubt among the public. The media duly publicizes the cases, amplifying doubt regarding the true winner. While justice grinds slowly through the courts, the state legislature notes that the "safe harbor date" is approaching, the date by which states must have certified their elections to avoid opening the door to a Congressional challenge to the election results. Needing to send a slate of electors, the state legislature cites all the media coverage of a doubted election, as well as the cases in court, and chooses the disputed side. The other, supposedly winning party files a case disputing the decision—but when the case hits the Supreme Court, justices support the independent state legislature theory they decided in favor of in June 2023, claiming that state legislatures have the final say in election determinations. Having moved past the safe harbor deadline, Congress has no recourse.

In the ensuing year, with control of both houses of Congress, the presidency, and majorities of state legislatures, partisans could alter voting rules at the national and state levels to solidify their gains. Over the next decade, voters see that they have no clout in states where their opposing votes do not count. Many move, as the personal realities created by the overturning of Roe v. Wade and child services interfering in the families of LGBTQ children cause Democrats to further concentrate themselves in states with legislation that favors their values, while Republicans angered by red tape on their businesses and annoyed by their children returning from school with homework on race and climate change do the same.

Businesses cowed by retaliatory legislation try to keep their voices out of politics in order to do business across state lines, allowing themselves to be increasingly extorted for campaign donations to avoid being punished for trumped-up political offenses. Others choose the partisan side most closely resembling their customer base. They limit their workforce and company headquarters to a state with their politics and remain outspoken about their values—at the cost of massive customer loss and a more limited market.

The result of these voting law changes, movements of people, and partisan gerrymandering, alongside the constitutional requirements of the electoral college and Senate representation, is that Democrats can no longer realistically win the presidency or a majority in the Senate, and they are blocked from a majority in the House of Representatives at least until the next census. They would gerrymander and alter laws in return to solidify strength in states they control. States where one party controls all major offices and cannot realistically be unseated become the overwhelming reality. Corruption grows, as tends to occur in such anocracies, tilting the political and economic playing field toward favored businesses and families. Polarization between the states deepens.

A stable, one-party state due to voting law changes is currently the situation in Hungary, now ranked only "partially free" by Freedom House. In the United States, thirty-three states (twenty Republican, thirteen Democrat) are already governed by one party in control of both legislative chambers, the governorship, the secretary of state, and the attorney general. Not all of these seats are solidified, but 2022 redistricting has pushed more of them in that direction.

COUNTRIES RUN BY ONE POLITICAL PARTY WHOSE CONTROL IS UPHELD BY VIOLENCE
Voters in some counties of Arizona, Georgia, and Texas face armed intimidation in and around voting booths during the 2024 election. A Georgia court allows the state to take over the precinct of Atlanta and determine the outcome. In Texas and Michigan, courts convict poll workers trying to keep armed actors from polling locations—making vigilantes feel the state is on their side and increasing intimidation of voting officials. When the election is decided in favor of Republicans, the left does not believe it has been free or fair.
Protests engulf the country. In more than one Black-majority city, police violence against protestors takes on a racial element. Militias and white supremacists enter cities to purportedly protect businesses, as they did during the 2020 Black Lives Matter protests. But these armed groups have grown stronger and more accepted over the last four years. In some counties, sheriffs and police have deputized extremist groups to serve as law enforcement support.
Over the next four years, vigilante violence backed by state acquiescence becomes a feature of politics in many jurisdictions. As doxing and violent protests at homes become common, dissent is increasingly dangerous. Businesses also keep their heads down, not wanting to be targeted by violent protests. Some

partisans with means move somewhere more friendly to their party. But the roaring economies of Texas and Florida keep many Democrats in these and other red states, just as many Republicans remain on the booming coasts. Meanwhile, inflation, interest rates, and high housing prices prevent many from moving to where they would feel safer.

By the end of the decade, intimidation upholds the political order in various counties that lean red but still have a strong Democratic plurality. While violence is still unusual, threats and legal harassment are a feature of political life, and occasional vigilante violence is common enough and rarely punished. Liberals in purple and red districts tend to keep their politics to themselves to avoid armed confrontations or threats against their kids. This violent tinge to politics and the inability of liberals to safely campaign or even recruit volunteers mean that Republicans tend to win swing districts. Progressives concentrated in urban cities lack political clout nationally but have become far more left politically than the majority of U.S. citizens. Republicans and even many moderates fear losing their jobs, toxic cyber comments, harassment of their kids at school, or threatening protests at their homes if they voice heterodox ideas.

Americans of both political parties who find themselves on the wrong side of their partisan divide, and those in the exhausted majority, feel democracy has devolved into mob rule and is a sham.

India's politics of intimidation bears some resemblance to parts of this story; it is now rated only "partially free" by Freedom House. This is also similar to earlier eras in U.S. history, including both the unstable period in the early years of Jim Crow and later when the system began to unravel following the Brown v. Board of Education Supreme Court decision in 1954, when White Citizens' Councils blossomed to carry out their so-called massive resistance campaign.

Countries With Political Stalemates and Increased Criminal and Political Violence

Thousands of new election officials for the 2024 election had been summoned to their jobs by Bannon and motivated by fears of fraud. During the election season, large numbers of mistakes and problems occurred. Many may have been caused less by ideology than incompetence after the loss of experienced election professionals—others were perpetrated purposely because of fears of fraud. The sheer number of errors render elections in many counties suspect. Meanwhile, in retaliation for the United States sending weapons to Ukraine, Russia hacks the election systems in multiple states. While in 2016, Russia tried to meddle but found most state voter rolls protected, by 2024, outdated Microsoft 7 software that no longer received security updates was being used in most jurisdictions, making changing voter files simple. The one thing that unites the country after 2024 is that Americans don't trust the results if the party that they oppose won their state. Stop the Steal rallies on the right and counter rallies on the left pop up in state after state. In big cities, protests are "protected" by left-wing militias whose ideologies, improvised weaponry, and refusal to engage with the police in pre-protest planning result in more brutal police tactics. The ensuing arrests and police brutality engender further protests that become increasingly violent at night. Militias and white supremacists eagerly enter the fray, using the street fights to hone their skills and recruit members.

As racial tensions and distrust rise, the police retreat from some areas. Meanwhile, their time is diverted from normal law enforcement to patrol protests and political events. Criminal violence rises. Murders, which jumped 30 percent in 2020 and rose again in 2021, increase further. Nationally, overwhelmed and less-trusted police have trouble solving cases, and fewer than half of all cases are solved, further increasing the murderous spiral. Social norms begin to break down under the strain. Road rage and other minor incidents turn increasingly deadly. Riots, protests, and lack of customers hurt businesses. Spending on security and reduced customer traffic increase costs and decrease revenue. While online stores bustle, city centers become hollow shells.

Politics remains competitive in many places. Politicians of both parties have a real chance, and voter intimidation is not commonplace. But candidates can virtually expect death threats, bricks in their windows, and the need to hire private security—most people think it's insane to run for office.

This situation has echoes of the 1960s and 1970s, when assassinations, riots, and the growth in fringe extremist groups affected trust and the zeitgeist of acceptability, leading to a doubling of the murder rate, which continued to rise until it hit an all-time high in the early 1990s. This is also a situation similar to Italy's Years of Lead. In 2020, the United States faced the greatest one-year rise in murder in over one hundred years; the rate rose further in 2021, and the clearance rate for homicides is already below 50 percent.

Americans are living with immense amounts of anger, hate, disdain, and fear. No one wants to live with these emotions, and no one wants to be on the receiving end. Society has driven itself into a corner from which there is nowhere to go.

But these trend lines are not etched in stone. Prognosticating forward from the 1880s would have led to three similar scenarios—some of which became true in the South. But a major, national, political and social movement brought about more honest politics, an end to child labor, safe food and water, and the flourishing of unions alongside business growth, heralding what became known as the American century. The 1960s and 1970s featured social unrest, thousands of nighttime bombings, the assassinations of multiple political leaders, and riots that hollowed out city centers for decades. And yet new policies, from post-Watergate political reforms to improved policing, had positive effects including reduced polarization, historically low levels of violence, and more productive politics, all of which held for nearly fifty years. Those reforms helped America usher in the internet, win the Cold War, and assist the greatest international florescence of democracy the world has ever seen.

Americans today can do better now than patching holes in our leaking ship. We can choose to be more creative to advance a far better future for all of us.

The five strategies described here aim at the roots of our acute problem: an alliance on the right between elites trying to consolidate power through antidemocratic means and an angry, illiberal social movement. This confluence means that democracy's problems must be tackled from both political and societal angles. A solution must also address the long-term challenges of those on the left who have given up on democracy. Finally, it must counter forces on both the left and right contributing to the pernicious polarization that makes solving democratic challenges so intractable, offering instead a positive, attractive, comforting vision in which all parts of the nation can see themselves as potentially gaining through its mutual creation.

Each of the tactics is a field unto itself; I do not intend to downplay the work involved. One goal of this paper is to show how much more expansive a true democracy agenda needs to be. Some areas, such as enabling responsible conservatives to vote for democracy and Electoral Count Act reform, are urgent. But others are of vital importance: without a coordinated and inclusive pro-democracy movement, for instance, all of the efforts to strengthen accountability and reset norms on what behavior is legal and acceptable will be dismissed as partisan and most will fail or even enhance polarization. The pernicious effects of U.S. democratic decline will not be confined to America's borders. As autocratic coordination increases, stumbles within U.S. democracy gravely harm democracy abroad. Given the strong correlations between democracy and economic growth through improved human capital, peace, and even life expectancy, a major setback to U.S. democracy would have tremendous consequences on global poverty and well-being.

The stakes are massive, and each moment deepens the polarization that is making these problems less amenable to change. As Americans, we must start now, at scale, strategically, with a broad, cross-party coalition to save our democracy.

Correction: The text has been updated to reflect that Jeff Flake chose not to run for reelection. Also, Cawthorn, Greene, and Boebert were elected in 2020, not 2018.

BUILD A BROAD-BASED, MULTI STRAND, PRO DEMOCRACY MOVEMENT AROUND A POSITIVE VISION CONCRETIZED IN LOCALLY ROOTED ACTION

More than half of all Americans believe the country's best days are behind them as a nation. Many feel the system is corrupt and not worth saving. Serious, positive, pro democracy work is currently confined to a small circle of people who are disproportionately middle to upper class, White, and talk mainly to each other. Yet international democracy-support research is crystal clear: mobilizing major change in polarized democracies requires broad-based constituencies of unlikely allies. International examples suggest that people are motivated by positive messages and concrete actions. In the context of U.S. democracy, eschewing national messages and issues in favor of local change is the best way to build on the trust that remains in the system and to evade partisan polarization.

Decades of international work to support democracy have found that broad-based social movements are the key to overturning authoritarian systems and that their strength lies not just in numbers but also in their breadth across polarized divides. America maintains a democracy, which is why the electoral components of enabling responsible conservatives to vote for democracy remain so important. But Americans can draw lessons from movements that have succeeded against more authoritarian odds.

Ideological partisanship is not the only divide that must be overcome to build a united, pro democracy movement.

All government systems rely on pillars of support to maintain legitimacy, such as the business community, religious leaders, the media, police, and the military. These pillars are composed of individuals with complex personal goals, identities, and needs. Movements to support democracy need to get more of these pillars to vocally join the pro democracy side and eschew active, or more often passive, support for antidemocratic activities. Attracting key individuals and groups within various pillars to stand publicly on the side of democracy signals to mainstream society that they, too, can stand for pro democracy goals without fear of retaliation. It is also essential for overcoming the polarization that allows authoritarianism to grow with voter support.

Ideological partisanship is not the only divide that must be overcome to build a united, pro democracy movement. Many indicators of democratic health in America move in different directions based on race, class, or age. For example, trust is a society's immune system, and it enables communities to unite against threats and come together to solve problems. Political trust in institutions is based on social trust, or a belief that others will follow publicly understood social norms and that broad values and expectations of each other are shared.

The decline in trust in democratic institutions and in fellow Americans over the last sixty years (with a sharp acceleration over the last twenty) is well documented. What is less known is that trust in government actually bottomed out under Obama, hitting just 5 percent and 6 percent for the so-called silent and boomer generations, respectively. But for Black Americans, it was rising at the moment when it was at rock-bottom for White Americans, who remain the demographic majority. Ominously, Black and White peoples' trust levels in government started moving in opposite directions at that time and have continued to do so—suggesting that policies and politicians who enhance the trust of one group are lowering the trust of another. Americans cannot build broad-based trust without bridging this racial divide.

Meanwhile Gen Z has the lowest level of trust of any generation and far less attachment to democracy. They need to be brought into the pro democracy space with efforts that are particular to their generation. This may entail civic education with international and historic examples of just what more can be lost and positive examples of what can be accomplished with broad-based action.

Finally, one of the few issues that unites Americans across parties is the widely held view that the system as a whole is rigged toward elites. This "vertical polarization" gets less attention than left-right polarization, but it is just as acute, has enabled populist politicians to gain ground, and causes democracy messaging to fall flat for audiences who feel that the so-called democracy is actually tilted against them.

Unifying a pro democracy movement must thus work not only across parties but across racial, generational, and class-cultural divides, while bringing in key societal pillars, such as businesses, religious institutions, and the military. It also must speak to divisions within these groups. Many racial minorities are progressive in some areas but hold more traditional religious beliefs, and many immigrants are both racial minorities and believe they can rise to the top of America through hard work and do not wish to solidify outsider identities.

Pro Democracy movement must be grounded in a positive vision of what the country could be Authoritarians rely on division—their strategy is to use fear and anger to divide society in order to get different parts of society on their side or at least to feel conflicted enough to remain passive. Deepening divisions, even for discrete pro democratic ends, thus helps the authoritarian playing field. Yet deepening and sharpening divisions is precisely what most partisan, get-out-the-vote messaging does. International experience in building broad-based movements, as well as U.S.-based efforts to fight disinformation, misinformation, and malinformation show that it's easier to mobilize with a negative vision—but that it is not enough to sustain success. Manifold movements with "Enough!" in their names have won battles against authoritarian governments globally, only to lose their democracies to backlash when they try to consolidate a new system absent a positive, inclusive vision. Even when pro democracy candidates and issues win using negative or fear-based messaging, it deepens polarization and thus invites backlash that entrenches the authoritarian playing field and enhances the authoritarian advantage over time. And when they lose, they increase nihilism and hopelessness.

A pro democracy movement must be grounded in a positive vision of what the country could be if everyone could see themselves and their children as benefiting in the future, rather than a zero-sum game to be won. In the same way that the efforts mentioned in the previous two sections could help White, right-wing men leaning toward extremism and could also assist African American men disaffected with decades of systematic mistreatment, some of the cure for the country's democratic ills requires recognizing where complex identities and needs intersect. These ideas and feelings must be concretized in images, grounded in philosophy and policy ideas, and made real through actions.

Finally, local methods of engagement help people gain agency and stay grounded in what is clearly real—not what nationalized media tells them is happening. Some of this engagement will entail local changes to the ways democracy is practiced. But pro-democracy work cannot be entirely political, otherwise it self-limits to a small slice of the citizenry who cares about politics. Americans must be reminded of what it means to come together and how that feels, through positive, apolitical group pursuits that offer moments of collective emotion— sports, concerts, community service, dance. These are all ways to emotionally engage Americans who may be too polarized to participate in pro-democracy activities in the political sphere or who may simply not be interested in politics.

Movement Building

Build a movement that brings together unlikely allies. Right and left, minorities and law enforcement, evangelical Christians and nonreligious individuals, younger Americans and older voters, businesses and unions—all of them need to be positive, active or passive parts of a broad-based, pro-democratic social movement in which members of every group can see themselves participating.

To bring together unlikely allies without losing flanks, as much work must be done to craft intraparty and intragroup solidarity for democracy as is dedicated to cross-group efforts. A conservative pro democracy movement must not be branded as anticonservative; a liberal pro democracy movement cannot be viewed as sacrificing core progressive goals. Liberals and conservatives who come together for democracy cannot simply be in the centers of their parties or come from one generation or race.

While on the right, intraparty work already omits violent individuals who have placed themselves on the antidemocratic side, on the left, more work is needed to address those willing to tolerate violence against businesses, personal property, and law enforcement. Research on broad-based movements shows that they must absolutely eschew violence of any type, even from aligned movements or flanks, because it quickly turns mainstream sentiment against them and reduces their breadth. Careful engagement must take place with groups that might otherwise use violence to achieve their ends.

Efforts to bring together intragroup and cross-group coalitions for democracy, build trust, and eventually engage in public actions will often be slow and under the radar; trust takes time and can be harmed by too much early public scrutiny. Despite slow returns on investment, these conferences, meetings, strategy sessions, and other trust-building and coalition-building activities are essential.

Narrative, Vision, and Philosophy

Craft a positive, forward-looking, inclusive vision of America that provides a place for all Americans while gaining precedence over divisive visions on the right and left. This is not a recommendation about communications alone—Americans must first believe in a positive future as a single country and then articulate and imagine that future before they can communicate it.

Tyranny requires the consent of those tyrannized—Putin controls Russia because many Russians believe nothing can be changed and that nihilism is the only reasonable response. People like Ukrainian President Volodymyr Zelenskyy are so dangerous to Putin's regime because they show people that a better path is possible. The United States is not facing tyranny but the hopelessness of fighting fellow Americans to a stalemate. For good reason, the pro democracy community is barely able to think beyond avoiding a stolen election in 2024. But as important as that goal is, it is hardly something to look forward to. Many Americans are demoralized by crime, inflation, and the fear of a downwardly mobile future for their children; they also cannot envision what the American dream looks like for them. Recent Supreme Court rulings are deepening polarization. A zero-sum, scarcity mindset cannot craft a way out of polarization and sclerosis.

Narratives must offer a common, hopeful view of America in which all Americans can see themselves as potentially successful, comfortable, and possessing agency and voice. A future vision cannot be blind to identity: women, racial minorities, and other identity groups band together because they know identity solidarity is essential to being heard in a world that remains normed to White, Christian men. But it must alter the thin notions of static, divided identities now in vogue on the far left and far right and instead center the multiplicity of identities within each person.

Today, an identity-obsessed far-right trumpets exclusion and an identity-focused far-left claims inclusion, but both offer a vision of a society based on a hierarchy of static, thin, and unchangeable identity markers in which some groups are on top and those who lack a privileged identity cannot aspire to greater status. What differs is simply where groups are positioned relative to each other, who has voice, and who is silenced. The status loss and reduction of agency that this zero-sum model of identity requires from certain groups is fueling backlash and empowering white nationalist identity movements and antidemocratic activities. Meanwhile, rather than unifying the country against a white supremacist vision of America, the fear of status loss is dividing the potential prodemocracy movement and pitting subgroups against one another.

Eric Ward, the executive director of the Western States Center, explains this best in an interview I recommend in its entirety:

I reject the recent trend of blaming [minority] communities for empowering themselves. However, I also strongly reject the growing practice by many leaders within minority communities to treat identity politics as a final destination. It's not. Identity politics are supposed to be our bridge to rebuilding people centered movements for justice . . . The problem with strengthening [static] narratives that force people into a position where their only identity is only white, or male, or a woman, or a Jew, or Black is that it strips them of the fullness of their humanity. It simply doesn't speak to who we are as humans. . . .

Being subjugated to the role of an ally, ensures that we'll never build a large enough movement or common identity that is viable enough to defeat systems of white supremacy or an emerging white nationalist movement. All we will do is leave inequality firmly entrenched.

These missteps increase the ability for more reactionary individuals to expand their attacks on civil rights and other people centered movements.

A future-centered image of what America could be must allow people to exist in the fullness of their identities—and to bring those contradictions and complexities into a modern America in which no one is automatically barred from gaining status because of any portion of their identity. What does an America look like where this occurs? Answering that question requires engaging it directly within and across groups to build a united pro democracy movement.

It is also important to consider what the pro democracy community is doing that may be at cross-purposes with building this vision. Organizations and philanthropists should speak up if the rhetoric and imagery that the groups they support are using supports a hierarchical image of society with static, unchangeable, thin identities—even if those images turn the traditional hierarchy on its head.

Invest in a multitude of arenas to build a new vision. A positive vision must be imagined and believed before it can be shared. This requires far more than focus groups and strategic communications. Americans who are exhausted, angry, and cut off from one another do not have the capacity to consider a better future, while the pro-democracy community is too focused on defending the democracy that exists, largely in its more abstract, institutional form, to think big.

It may seem Pollyannaish at the current moment to consider a future together. Yet the alternative to a future together is one that somehow is lived apart. While some on the right trumpet secession, and some on the left would be happy to see them go, such a path is not only impractical and potentially deadly but also simply allows the same cultural and political problems to continue in the same places, under a different national name. There is simply no other way forward but to craft a joint future. In postconflict settings, the international community asks countries to integrate people who have massacred, stolen from, beaten, and tortured their fellow citizens back into communities and villages. Are Americans so much smaller-hearted and unimaginative that partisans cannot envision ways to live together with those with whom divisions are not yet as stark?

The visions Americans must build should not be about the abstraction of democracy itself—they should be about what Americans hope for from their daily life in America. This future lived experience must be concrete and grounded. Perhaps deliberative democracy exercises could be used to discuss different parts of daily life, as well as major culture-war issues, to diffuse the latter with ideas that undermine hardened polarization with practical thinking while elevating shared desires for Americans' lives in the future. How does the country achieve the American Dream of the future, together, rather than by looking back nostalgically at an America in which portions of the population were kept from competing or offering a vision that frightens the people who remain the majority of the voting public? Figuring that out is major work in and of itself.

Develop a cohesive philosophy and grounding ideas. A narrative of a future that crosses the chasms of partisan polarization and the polarization between elites and non elites must also be supported by philosophical, policy, and intellectual efforts that offer depth. How would and should policies change if there were not a dominant, assumed, normative identity in the United States? What would change in the economic system to support an America of greater opportunity in rural areas as well as cities and for the non-college-educated? How can the philosophical values of "freedom from" and "freedom for" both be instantiated? What core values underpin such a vision, what values are undermined, and how are these values grounded in the country's founding documents, religious texts, and other places Americans go for meaning and moral absolutes? Do current efforts to group and enumerate subcommunities help or hinder complex identities, and how could Americans do better while also meeting other public service needs? How would work to move these ideas forward upend assumptions within racial, religious, or other communities of interest that might generate backlash, and what could help them find footing? These are questions best answered by think tanks, special editions of serious magazines, and public intellectuals. They need conferences and core support to answer these questions in conversation with one another within and across societal divides.

Disseminate these ideas. Dissemination will require artistic, literary, and cultural endeavors as well as advertising and other mass-media efforts to inculcate a concrete, pictorial vision of what a more inclusive America, with complicated identities and a greater agency for individuals, looks like and can be. For instance, just as advertisers are shaping images of healthy masculinity, advertisers could be brought into communication with pro democracy groups and narrative specialists to see what ideas bubble up from focus groups aimed at many demographics, while testing what forms of rhetoric and imagery can catch the public imagination and counter the current great replacement theory trope that pits one group of Americans against another. To enhance the stability of the country, the Chamber of Commerce and other business groups might consider supporting public service announcements and online campaigns that reinforce this complex, positive, future-oriented vision of America.

Journalism should also be involved, by supporting reporting and editing that complicates narratives and brings full individuals with complex identities more clearly into view for the American public.

Local, Concrete Action

Ideas and images must be concretized in lived experience. The progressive movement was successful in part because it had many strands through which people could engage—from building local playgrounds to prison reform, ranked choice voting to antitrust activities, where Americans could act within their neighborhoods or at the national level. Even abstract politics was rooted in local associations to get things done. Viewed purely from a methods perspective, progressive strategies of building broad-based and active coalitions that connected democratic reforms to social engagement and local action are worth emulating. Reinvigorate local politics. Americans are frustrated by problems that are not getting solved and by national narratives that obscure complexities, deepen polarization, and prevent communities from addressing obvious needs. Particularly in places facing significant social dislocation, rapidly changing demographics, economic downturn, or speedy economic growth and inequality, communities need to be engaged in practical solutions to real problems. The local level, where trust remains highest, is where people can build civic attitudes and habits from such engagement. Local engagement on issues that matter locally, if well-massaged and moderated, can help people exercise problem-solving muscles.

For instance, the furor over schools and curricula is one of many issues that has been politicized into binary caricatures, with debates fueled by national groups, such as Moms for Liberty, that are backed with national money and a national agenda. But the intensity points to deep demand across the political aisle for solutions. Many parents—who are being pushed toward extremes or silenced—actually hold mixed, complex views, from those who saw their kids' educational attainment and mental health suffering during prolonged school closures to those frustrated by what they saw during Zoom classes. Engagements modeled after Democracy in One Room, which brought together hundreds of Americans in a representative sample to discuss tough issues in a moderated manner with factual information brought in throughout, could reduce the shouting and give parents a means to improve their kids' lives and understand what their schools and teachers are dealing with.

Such deliberative democracy models might meet Americans in multiple arenas where they are already passionate and could assist in finding common-sense solutions that defang cultural wedge issues. Like schooling, climate change is a national, polarized issue. But many communities are increasingly affected by fires, floods, or tornadoes, and they can engage in concrete ways to build resilience to these disasters locally. A multitude of other issues can enable people to practice their problem-solving muscles in actual situations in which they must address the complexities of others' lives and desires, reducing the national caricatures that others have become.

Localities can experiment with a variety of new democratic methods to increase engagement, from participatory budgeting (such as when Madrid allocated 100 million euros of its municipal budget through citizen rankings of projects in order of preference), to citizen assemblies (which in Ireland have been used to recommend constitutional and legislative referendums on issues from abortion to the structure of Dublin's local government). In Europe, the International Observatory on Participatory Democracy collects examples of these practices that the United States could look to for ideas. Increase healthy, cohesive local social engagements. Narrative must be embodied in experience. But America has been on a decades-long path of reduced social engagement. Community engagement in and of itself is not necessarily good—a study of Weimar Germany found that Nazi membership grew more quickly in places with more dense community organizations. In the United States, greater white evangelical church attendance and right-wing engagement with community groups is correlated with higher levels of belief in conspiracy theories.

Instead, social engagements that bridge differences in ways that unite people in common tasks are important. However, many bridging programs, as they are often called, have deep flaws: they self-select people with the time and ideological preferences that make them open to such engagement, thus failing to reach target audiences. They often push toward a mealy middle that fails to honor different identities or respect real differences. And by asking people to show up in their opposing identities, they risk reifying and hardening identities of partisanship or other differences. Many rely on conversation alone, which research suggests is inadequate for success, rather than a constructive task. Instead, what is needed is:

Eschew bridging divides for their own sake, and embraces self-help for mutual benefit.

Americans need to engage across their divides. But self-conscious bridging-divides programs leave out both more partisan and less political Americans. These key groups are more likely to engage in organizations that give them some benefit than those that are explicitly about healing our nation. Unions once provided skilled laboring men, in particular, with social engagements that crossed partisan lines. Unions are unique in that the choice to invest time in a disparate group of people with whom one shares little in common other than a job also helps the giver directly. Civic commitments that include this sort of self-help are likely to have more staying power and reach people who are pressed for time or otherwise uninterested in cross-partisan or cross-racial engagement.

In addition to unions, some of the largest examples of such cross-partisan engagement for mutual benefit today are the various twelve-step groups for alcoholics, addicts to narcotics, and similar groups that maintain that the opposite of addiction is connection. Deeply personal, locally based meetings involve high levels of personal engagement where partisan identity is unimportant while the shared identity of overcoming addiction bridges divides. Sadly, opioid use has now crossed racial and class barriers, making such groups a major way that Americans of all types meet and build community. What if part of the connection such groups fostered was connection to our civic fabric, adding a positive sense of agency and the empowerment of community service to interpersonal healing?

Lending circles—an updated form of the old mutual aid and burial associations in which a group of people meet regularly to divide funds, take loans, and help one another with entrepreneurial ventures—are common in other countries. They are just getting started in the United States, where they can build community, help people with essential financial support, and build credit for the one-third of American adults who have low credit scores or no credit history.

Other forms of mutual self-help are myriad: sports and recreation groups for adults or families could also be encouraged with the provision of civic space, creation of tournaments, and volunteer opportunities for trail building, field improvements, and other material outcomes. Religion is among the most racially and partisan divided spaces in the nation—what if the desire for connection with the divine was brought together with the need to connect across differences? Construction, landscaping, and gardening mutual help groups might be assisted with a tool lending library, city- or private-sponsorship of occasional how-to classes, and civic space and encouragement. By assisting these efforts but requiring volunteer time in return, cities will actually reap greater civic benefit than if they overly provide for these efforts.

Bringing people together across social groupings should be a goal of these programs, based on research that finds creating a third identity in a constructive engagement together is one of the best ways to alter perceptions and polarization. But to garner participation from those most in need of it, these programs should not be framed as overtly about democracy or politics; the goal is to build other forms of social problem-solving and community engagement that breaks partisan barriers and instead unites across differences.

Invest in social activities that simply remind people that they enjoy doing things as a community. Mayors should be encouraged to hold a variety of civic days for engagement with low barriers to entry and time commitments that can range from little to greater, including community concerts, movies, clean-up days, family sports days, and civic festivals that require engagement, such as Mardi Gras in New Orleans.

To build on ideas mentioned earlier, events that specifically target men should be front and center, such as father-child sporting events, coaching opportunities, rebuilding the homes of the elderly, or Habitat for Humanity–style activities that offer men the chance to play positive, respected roles in their communities. Because of the level of geographic partisan sorting, such events will likely do little to bridge partisan divides. Instead, they are attempts to help people facing loneliness, anomie, and personal dislocation find positive communities that tie them to American ideals, rather than leaving them to build negative online associations that pull them toward violence.

Engage social urbanism. Wherever possible, such events should encourage mixing from different parts of municipalities to bridge class and racial divides. For example, in Medellin, Colombia, an effort to fight violence included holding popular city concerts in lower-income parts of the city to encourage a common civic identity. Also, desirable civic infrastructure—such as a library built by an internationally renowned architect—was built in less desirable parts of town to restitch the civic fabric.

The United States should consider such "social urbanism" concepts to use urban planning to benefit democracy. After all, thinkers from former president Thomas Jefferson to French historian Alexis de Tocqueville recognized the value of town squares in New England as embodying and assisting the country's nascent democracy. What would a geography of place look like that assisted democracy and reduced the barriers created by the current levels of inequality? This is a question that could be seeded in urban planning conferences and universities.

Craft community and municipal resilience strategies. Communities like Whitefish, Montana have used replicable strategies to face down hate and bring their communities together. The DOJ's Community Relations Service, the Federal Mediation and Conciliation Service, and nonprofits should be supported in their efforts to work with local officials and leaders within states and municipalities to create early warning and response systems that convene groups across differences—including religious organizations, businesses, trusted local media, local government, and other stakeholders—to dampen rumors and address threats in particular localities or communities where tensions are high or where data or trends indicate the likelihood of greater tension. Support for the DOJ's Community Relations Service should be expanded so that it can broaden its role in training communities and law enforcement in methods to keep the peace, address hate crimes, and develop ongoing, sustainable, community-based methods to prevent and respond to violence fueled by hate, while nonprofits with mediation experience can assist in broadening its reach.

STRENGTHEN ACCOUNTABILITY TO RESET NORMS ON WHAT BEHAVIOR IS LEGAL AND ACCEPTABLE

A strategy to support democracy requires sticks as well as carrots. There are red lines that must be upheld for democracy to work. Those who lose elections have to accept defeat. Those who interfere in elections must be denounced and brought to account. Violence can have no place in democratic life. Corruption poisons trust—whether corrupt actions are technically legal or not. Politicians and wealthy elites cannot be above the laws that bind the rest of the people.

it is crucial to have a united and cross-party democracy movement of unlikely allies to engage in and support accountability together.

Accountability from the state and from society matters in determining what is viewed as acceptable political and social behavior and what is unthinkable. The more laws must be brought to bear, the more the rule of law will be strained—for that reason, wherever possible, it is better to assert social norms to curb antidemocratic behavior. However, as these social norms give way, the legal net below is too threadbare to catch the free fall of U.S. democracy. It needs shoring up.

Accountability must be carefully deployed to avoid backlash. In other countries, when state actions to quell violent uprisings like the militia movement in the United States castanet broad enough to include innocents or involve state violence in return, the result is the growth of the very movements that governments are trying to squelch. Because the actions below to hold people to account can be falsely construed as antidemocratic by the fraction of Americans who believe that their efforts to counter election fraud and authoritarian pandemic mandates are fighting for democracy, it is crucial to have a united and cross-party democracy movement of unlikely allies to engage in and support accountability together. The more cross-ideological pillars of support to back these norms, the harder they will be to dismiss as partisan.

Reform the Electoral Count Act . This law from the post–Civil War period determines the final decision regarding national elections, and it is full of dangerous loopholes. As former federal circuit judge J. Michael Luttig articulated during the Select Committee on January 6 hearings, it needs rapid reform to clarify procedures in order to avoid democratic disaster in the case of a close election in 2024. Reform of the Electoral Count Act must be prioritized even if a broader set of desirable reforms turn out to be impossible.

Use civil impact litigation to try to bankrupt and deter violent and extreme antidemocratic groups. This strategy has been used against the Unite the Right and January 6 rally organizers; individuals who have engaged in intimidation and violence, like the founder of the neo-Nazi website Daily Stormer; and media organizations such as the Gateway Pundit and One America News Network that appear to assist in the spread of violence and disinformation.

Pursue criminal lawsuits against individuals who undertake violence, threaten officials, or break democratic laws. While criminal law is the purview of the government, outside organizations can help states understand and use lesser-known laws, and philanthropy can assist these groups.

Bring lawsuits against government bodies to force them to uphold equality under the law, protect rights, and avoid misuse of government services. These lawsuits are particularly important to bring against law enforcement bodies to convince voters that laws will be applied equally and will protect all. For example, there are important lawsuits against the Department of Homeland Security following its federal deployment of riot police in Portland and against local Texas police who refused to assist calls for help as a Biden campaign convoy was attacked by pro-Trump drivers.

Ensure professional accountability , such as being disbarred, for lawyers who violate democratic norms. Other professional norm-setting bodies and entities should be used to hold members accountable and uphold democratic norms.

Bring legal challenges and support legal scholars to build and advance long-term legal theories that enhance prodemocratic norms. Some of this work will be defensive, such as undermining efforts to enshrine the independent state legislature theory that is being revived despite the significant violence it enabled around elections throughout the nineteenth century. Other aspects must be forward-looking, to build the legal foundation for an economy of greater opportunity, for example, or to ground group and individual rights in a manner that enables greater identity complexity.

Clarify state and federal laws and doctrine against violence to make them easier to adjudicate or to enable greater deterrence. Measures could include:

extending protections against intimidation from election officials to immediate family members, contractors, and vendors;

extending the doctrine to strengthen the rules against extremism within the active-duty military to the laws that govern federal law enforcement, particularly at the Department of Homeland Security and the Department of Justice; and

clarifying legal conditions and precedent to remove extremists in local law enforcement.

Increase accountability for political elites and white-collar criminals. The sense that the wealthy are buying American politics is widespread and corrosive to trust in democracy—both Biden and Trump voters listed accountability for public leaders as their fifth most important value in an in-depth survey.

Often these concerns are translated into efforts to curb money in politics. Such work is currently doomed, given the composition of the Supreme Court and precedents on money equaling speech. Moreover, efforts to limit campaign spending can backfire: plutocratic money will always find a way to affect the system when big issues that affect businesses or wealthy ideologues are on the table. Meanwhile, small-dollar donors are not necessarily better for democracy: small-dollar donations tend to support anti establishment candidates, which means they also support more polarizing candidates on the left and right. Small-dollar donations surged after January 6 when some corporations temporarily cut funding to candidates who supported the insurrection. The most extreme Republican candidates, such as Greene, bought expensive fundraising lists and used them to fundraise from small-dollar donors while building an image of widespread grassroots appeal. Meanwhile, limiting donation amounts leads candidates to waste inordinate time on fundraising, forcing them to spend more time with wealthy givers. Their lack of time leads them to lean even more on lobbyists for policy information, allowing money to influence policy through even more direct routes than donations.

Thus, a more orthogonal approach focused on accountability for the wealthy and well-connected instead of on campaign donations may achieve more while meeting the actual desires of more Americans for accountability of elites. Although overt corruption in America is quite low, the sense that the system is rigged is in part based on legal activities that feel unfair to many Americans—such as the ability of corporations and wealthy individuals to avoid taxes. It has not been lost on the American public that financial elites impoverished millions in 2008, with few repercussions, or that much of the campaign support that is legally allowed in America feels corrupt. Nearly three-quarters of Americans are somewhat or very dissatisfied with the influence of major corporations on democracy (though, crucially, nearly the same amount trust small business). Increasing taxes for the extremely wealthy, closing loopholes for them and for corporations, and other activities that make people believe that plutocrats are paying their share and abiding by the same laws are crucial for enhancing the public's belief in the democratic system.

One step is shining light on the problem—but internationally, transparency without change can actually enhance the public's view that their political system is rigged. Therefore, efforts to reduce corruption and legal activities that appear to benefit political and financial elites must not only shine light but also enhance actual accountability and repercussions. This has been made harder by the Supreme Court, but the issue is not as intractable as campaign finance reform is.

Pursue Supreme Court term limits. While courts still enjoy higher levels of trust than U.S. politicians and electoral institutions, the overturning of Roe v. Wade after multiple justices declared the case as settled precedent in front of Congress feels to many on the left like perjury before Congress, which is itself a crime. The lack of ethics rules also undermines trust. Recent court decisions also enable political corruption, further undermining faith in the democratic system.

Until the 1960s, the average tenure of a supreme court justice was fifteen years; it is now twenty-six years. Majorities of both parties support limiting the tenure of

Supreme Court justices—in May 2022, term limits garnered 60 percent support—even as they disagree about adding justices to the court's number. There is historical precedent in which to ground a change to tenure and service. At the country's founding, Supreme Court judges "rode circuit," which meant serving simultaneously as Supreme Court and lower federal court judges. These roles were only separated in the 1800s by an act of Congress, not a constitutional amendment. Biden's Presidential Commission on the Supreme Court of the United States has a long discourse regarding the possibility of returning to such an arrangement based on federal judges serving eighteen-year-long Supreme Court stints with term limits, which would allow each president to choose an equal number of justices each term. While such a change would be seen as political in the current moment, it might assist in depoliticizing court confirmations and lowering the stakes over the long term. Meanwhile, ethics rules for the Supreme Court are wise and extremely popular.

COMMON STRATEGIES THAT ARE INSUFFICIENT TO ALTER THE TRAJECTORY OF U.S. DEMOCRACY

American democracy is starting to drown.
Philanthropists are investing in a number of strategies that are treading water. These are essential for keeping democracy alive and important to invest in. But they are not able to get the country out of the current situation.
In preparation for the 2024 elections, some philanthropists are crafting a multi-hundred-million-dollar

effort to protect the election. A similar effort in 2020 funded crucial activities that contributed to a free and fair election and potentially prevented an even more precipitous democratic decline that could have been predicted from a second Trump term. Without those efforts, democracy would be in a far worse place today. However, despite significant funds, such activities did not alter the negative trajectory of U.S. democracy. If anything, democratic decline has sped up at the state level. Because these strategies are major planks of pro-democracy activity and philanthropy, it is worth spelling out why they are necessary but insufficient to meet the challenge. For the foreseeable future, U.S. democracy will need a both-and, not an either-or, solution set.

Help Democrats win. A number of the theories below may be executed as good faith, nonpartisan strategies or may be pursued subconsciously or more explicitly to help Democrats win until the Republican Party becomes a prodemocratic party again. Given the revelations surrounding Trump's efforts to overturn a legitimate election in 2020, and the fact that many who aided his efforts on Capitol Hill and in some states are still in power, these strategies are important to forestalling more rapid democratic decline, especially if Trump runs in 2024.

However, a strategy grounded in helping Democrats win to save democracy is 100 percent certain to fail. In twenty states, Republicans already hold both legislative chambers and the roles of governor, attorney general, and secretary of state. Democrats cannot realistically alter state policies in these states through government control; they must change minds. Nationally, the constitutional framework—combined with strong national support for Republicans and the redistricting of seats in the House of Representatives that just occurred following the 2020 census and will last for the next decade—means that the Republican Party is very likely to win power over Congress and/or the presidency before it ends its current antidemocratic tactics. And perhaps most problematic for this strategy is experience: after 2020, Democrats won control of the presidency and both chambers of Congress—and democratic degradation nevertheless advanced rapidly at the state level and within society.

Meanwhile, the perception of partisan bias in pro democracy activities may be sharpening divisions and precluding efforts to bolster democracy.

Increase voter turnout. More Americans voted in 2020 than in any modern election. Both parties experienced significant gains. Meanwhile, the number of antidemocratic election law alterations at the state level grew, as did increases in violent threats, while trust in elections eroded greatly among Republicans and Independents.

Get more minorities to vote. This strategy often tries to marry the fact that challenges to voting disproportionately target minorities and that people of color have historically voted Democratic. However, by attempting to kill two birds with one stone, it risks missing both.

Targeting all the laws being passed to suppress voting fails to prioritize those that most harm both minorities and democracy. For instance, no state had voter identification requirements before 2006, making them a long-term focus of the democracy community hoping to help minority voters. While voter identification laws don't have overall effects on turnout, some studies suggest that they do suppress minority votes, particularly of Latinos. Other large, credible studies find no negative effect on any demographic group (nor any effect on fraud). Meanwhile, voter identification laws are supported by large majorities of Black voters (66 percent), Hispanic voters (77 percent), and Asian voters (75 percent), meaning that fighting battles to remove identification requirements yields equivocal outcomes that aren't supported by the communities that activists are purporting to help.

Similarly, I love mail-in voting and personally wrote in its support in multiple venues in 2020 because of its importance to an election held during a pandemic prior to vaccine availability. Mail-in ballots accounted for nearly half the 2020 ballots. But its use was miniscule before 2000—when U.S. democracy was in better shape. It largely expanded, for good reason, because of fears of large gatherings during a deadly, contagious pandemic. Meanwhile, there's no evidence behind claims that it benefits Democrats, and its record with improving minority turnout is mixed. (Though theoretically helpful for preventing problems with long election lines, fears of violence, or an inability to get time off from work on election day, African Americans tend to use it less, in part due to justified fears that their ballots will be disproportionately disqualified, while Hispanic or elderly voters use it the most).

Linking important voting measures that have public support with those that don't opens the entire agenda to questioning. To maintain credibility and focus, pro-democracy efforts to help minorities vote should target the rules that are empirically proven to have harmful effects such as longer wait times, caused in part by reduced Sunday voting and reduced voting locations. Ideally, they would target those that both have harmful effects and are felt by minority voters themselves to be most problematic.

For those pursuing minority votes in the hopes of increasing Democratic chances, the realities in crucial states such as Florida—which now comprises over a tenth of the votes for the electoral college—are becoming more mixed. Racial minorities have multiple identities: they may also be male, religious, working class, rural, or immigrants from communist nations, allowing their votes to be harnessed by politicians who can speak to other elements of their identities that may be more salient to them. Latino voters have never been a monolith. They showed more conservative voting patterns in the 2020 election than in 2016, and majorities of second-generation immigrants saw themselves as "typical Americans" in a reply to a survey question with that wording. Majorities of immigrants are more concerned with economic than social issues. And nearly ten percent of Black Americans are now immigrants, which is one potential reason for the increase in Black male votes for Trump—which reached nearly a third in high-immigration states like Minnesota. Among those who are immigrants from former communist countries, many have been targeted by disinformation, misinformation, and malinformation and are proponents of the "big lie," which implies that Trump actually won the 2020 election. Moreover, negative partisanship means that identity-based campaigns may increase turnout for the other side.

Court more swing voters. The alternative to a base-vote theory is a swing-voter theory. This is difficult, but not impossible, for moving voters away from Trump and other proponents of the big lie. The effort to court swing voters in partisan general elections through persuasion (as opposed to fielding a candidate who simply attracts this group) appears to rarely work without a strong ground game and other innovative tactics: there are just too few persuadable voters left, except in unusual races or with particularly careful targeting efforts. Persuadable voters do seem to move if they have been properly identified through experiments and then targeted with methods like real, face-to-face conversations. These efforts are worth engaging in for targeted races where they can make a difference. But very little of the money spent on persuasion actually goes to efforts shown to work: the vast majority is spent on advertising that has virtually no effect.

Meanwhile, for those wanting to move the country in a democratic direction rather than just voting for Democrats, there is another problem: the two groups of voters who are least likely to support democracy—those who have previously voted for different parties and those who do not vote consistently—also represent two key characteristics of swing voters. Swing voters show the strongest support for a third party—but not the one that many good-government types imagine. Only 4 percent of U.S. voters want a moderate party that is socially liberal and economically conservative. Instead, many support liberal economic redistribution combined with conservative cultural policies: they favor government help for themselves and others they deem "deserving" (a category with a strong racial tilt), combined with greater salience of a white, Christian, native-born identity, leaving them with a foot in both parties. Swing-voting White Americans—many of whom moved into the Republican Party in 2016—scored particularly high on racial resentment. Among these economic liberals and cultural conservatives, Democracy Fund's Voter Study Group found that 52 percent supported a "strong leader" who need not bother with Congress or elections, and 40 percent did not favor democracy.

Neither a sense of being left behind economically nor changes to individual economic standing are correlated with Trump voters. These findings echo multiple other studies of terrorism, right-wing violence, and the January 6 insurrectionists that find that poverty, the decline of manufacturing, unemployment, and other economic factors are not predictive of right-wing violence in the United States.

Improve the electoral system. U.S. elections have real security challenges, such as software so outdated that software providers have declared that they will discontinue patches before 2024, as well as problems born of normal human errors that provide ready fodder for disinformation and distrust. Rebuilding faith in the electoral system must include bipartisan, compromise measures that make voting more secure and more accessible, such as those passed in Kentucky in 2021. It also requires efforts to simply improve local election administration, such as the U.S. Alliance for Election Excellence is doing. These efforts are important and necessary—fighting alleged fraud that did not occur is hard enough; arguing for democracy in the face of actually compromised elections would be far more difficult and is a reality that the country would have faced in 2020 but for a massive infusion of private capital to allow counties to purchase protective gear, pay workers, and otherwise run the 2020 elections. Yet, technical reforms are not enough to alter the perceptions that are deliberately being seeded to undermine faith in elections. Colorado, for instance, has some of the nation's most technically proficient elections, as well as a virulent Stop the Steal movement. Facts don't alter beliefs. Meanwhile, the grants made in 2020 to make elections more secure actually fueled doubts in some people. Philanthropists hoping to use technical reform to actually strengthen election security are sensible. Those seeking to use such donations to strengthen belief in elections should look to the field of international development, where decades of research into using funding to strengthen government services in order to deepen government legitimacy show that such programs often enhance distrust, in part because they

are inevitably delivered earlier or in greater amounts to some communities that are themselves distrusted.
Increase economic redistribution. The acute degradation of U.S. democracy is not being caused by poverty, unemployment, or other causes of individual economic loss. Democracy Fund's Voter Study Group found no correlation between personal financial circumstances and support for authoritarianism. Neither a sense of being left behind economically nor changes to individual economic standing are correlated with Trump voters.. These findings echo multiple other studies of terrorism, right-wing violence, and the January 6 insurrectionists that find that poverty, the decline of manufacturing, unemployment, and other economic factors are not predictive of right-wing violence in the United States. Those most frustrated with democracy are facing a sense of thwarted expectation based on the gap between what they are achieving and what they believe themselves to be entitled to. Data internationally shows that such perceptions are fairly impervious to rising individual incomes. In fact, in the United States, more economically developed states are most at risk of right-wing violence. Internationally, some research suggests that extremist politics may be most attractive to people who are doing less well than others within a growing economy (even if they are doing better than they had been doing previously), making economic redistribution a poor tool to target the problem.
Reforms to help individuals improve economically are useful—if directed toward disadvantaged minority communities, where concrete economic programs could

address the democratic erosion caused by democracy's failure to deliver. But the victim narrative and grievance politics of the partisan right make doing so without backlash difficult, unless redistribution occurs across class lines. Meanwhile, for the reasons discussed earlier, economic redistribution programs will not address the drivers of democratic decline from the right. While government redistribution programs to individuals won't alleviate democratic challenges from the right, the economic structure of America is playing a role in enhancing status anxiety and allowing cultural issues that are stand-ins for class be weaponized for authoritarian ends. Economic shocks such as the 2008 recession do affect feelings toward the entire political system—particularly when the wealthy received bailouts and the working and middle classes did not. Inequality also enhances a sense of status loss and feelings that the system is rigged, as well as being highly correlated with violence. More work is needed in looking at what alterations to America's basic economic structure could help its democracy and what forms of implementation would work to concretize those goals.

Fix gerrymandering. The United States needs to have a serious conversation about gerrymandering. Allowing politicians to pick their constituents reduces trust in the system and enables the increase in safe seats that are driving extreme candidates.

Yet there are three problems with simply doing away with gerrymandering. First, it is easy to speak against partisan gerrymandering when the other side is doing it—but harder to defend unilateral disarmament.

Second, racial gerrymandering is allowed under the Voting Rights Act, and it helps minority voters symbolically and substantively. Yet racial gerrymanders are seen as partisan by the right. Paradoxically, they may harm overall Democratic chances for gaining seats in the House of Representatives by packing large numbers into safe districts above what is required for representation. Moreover, because their votes matter disproportionately to one party, gerrymandering allows the other party to ignore, suppress, or even engage in violence against minority voters, a pattern that plays out around the world and that leads some other divided societies to undertake vote-pooling systems like ranked choice. Finally, voter-supported legislation to reduce gerrymandering—such as Florida's laws requiring districts to be built around contiguous areas—can undermine political and racial gerrymandering, leading to calls of racial unfairness. And, of course, much of the problem of safe seats has to do with voters self-sorting geographically, not gerrymandering itself.

Something that seems to voters so blatantly unfair must be addressed—and yet the solution set here is unclear. The United States needs new thinking, not doubling down on the old.

THREE POSSIBLE FUTURES

America is approaching three possible futures in the near term. These are not far-off prognostications. Instead, they are intended to hold a mirror to a future that is almost here, to show what is likely to solidify. Without significant, fast action, America could start to look like other:

stable countries run by one political party where voters
cannot alter politics,
countries run by one political party whose control is
upheld by violence, or
countries with political stalemates and increased
criminal and political violence.

STABLE COUNTRIES RUN BY ONE POLITICAL PARTY WHERE VOTERS CANNOT ALTER POLITICS

Close elections in 2024 in states like Michigan,
Pennsylvania, or Wisconsin lead local activists from the
losing party to file allegations of fraud. Their goal is not
to win, necessarily, but to delay certification and sow
doubt among the public. The media duly publicizes the
cases, amplifying doubt regarding the true winner. While
justice grinds slowly through the courts, the state
legislature notes that the "safe harbor date" is
approaching, the date by which states must have
certified their elections to avoid opening the door to a
Congressional challenge to the election results. Needing
to send a slate of electors, the state legislature cites all
the media coverage of a doubted election, as well as the
cases in court, and chooses the disputed side. The
other, supposedly winning party files a case disputing
the decision—but when the case hits the Supreme
Court, justices support the independent state legislature
theory they decided in favor of in June 2023, claiming
that state legislatures have the final say in election
determinations. Having moved past the safe harbor
deadline, Congress has no recourse.

In the ensuing year, with control of both houses of Congress, the presidency, and majorities of state legislatures, partisans could alter voting rules at the national and state levels to solidify their gains. Over the next decade, voters see that they have no clout in states where their opposing votes do not count. Many move, as the personal realities created by the overturning of Roe v. Wade and child services interfering in the families of LGBTQ children cause Democrats to further concentrate themselves in states with legislation that favors their values, while Republicans angered by red tape on their businesses and annoyed by their children returning from school with homework on race and climate change do the same.

Businesses cowed by retaliatory legislation try to keep their voices out of politics in order to do business across state lines, allowing themselves to be increasingly extorted for campaign donations to avoid being punished for trumped-up political offenses. Others choose the partisan side most closely resembling their customer base. They limit their workforce and company headquarters to a state with their politics and remain outspoken about their values—at the cost of massive customer loss and a more limited market.

The result of these voting law changes, movements of people, and partisan gerrymandering, alongside the constitutional requirements of the electoral college and Senate representation, is that Democrats can no longer realistically win the presidency or a majority in the Senate, and they are blocked from a majority in the House of Representatives at least until the next census.

They would gerrymander and alter laws in return to solidify strength in states they control. States where one party controls all major offices and cannot realistically be unseated become the overwhelming reality. Corruption grows, as tends to occur in such anocracies, tilting the political and economic playing field toward favored businesses and families. Polarization between the states deepens.

A stable, one-party state due to voting law changes is currently the situation in Hungary, now ranked only "partially free" by Freedom House. In the United States, thirty-three states (twenty Republican, thirteen Democrat) are already governed by one party in control of both legislative chambers, the governorship, the secretary of state, and the attorney general. Not all of these seats are solidified, but 2022 redistricting has pushed more of them in that direction.

CONCLUSION

Fear, resentment, hatred, and a great deal of anger permeate American life.Nobody wants to experience these feelings for themselves or for others.Society has pushed itself into a bind that it cannot escape.

In any case, these pattern lines are not carved in stone.Three scenarios that were similar if predictions had been made forward from the 1880s would have occurred, some of which came to pass in the South.However, a significant national political and social movement heralded the beginning of what would become known as the American century by bringing about more honest politics, the end of child labor, safe food and water, and the flourishing of unions alongside business expansion.Social unrest, thousands of nighttime bombings, the assassination of multiple political leaders, and riots that decimated city centers for decades characterized the 1960s and 1970s.But new policies, from political reforms after Watergate to better policing, had positive effects like less polarization, historically low levels of violence, and more productive politics that lasted nearly 50 years.America was able to establish the internet, win the Cold War, and support the greatest ever international florescence of democracy as a result of those reforms.

Instead of patching holes in our ship that are leaking, Americans can do better right now.In order to make our collective futures much better, we can choose to be more creative.

The five approaches discussed here seek to address the root causes of our pressing issue:an alliance on the right between an irrational, illiberal social movement and elites attempting to cling to power through antidemocratic means.Because of this convergence, democracy's issues must be addressed from both a political and societal perspective.The long-term challenges faced by those on the left who have given up on democracy must also be addressed in a solution.Last but not least, it needs to combat forces on both the left and right that contribute to the harmful polarization that makes it so difficult to solve democratic problems.Instead, it needs to present a positive, inviting, and reassuring vision that all parts of the country can see themselves potentially benefiting from its mutual creation.

Each tactic is its own distinct field;I will not minimize the effort required.This paper aims to demonstrate how much more inclusive a true democracy agenda must be.Electoral Count Act reform and allowing responsible conservatives to vote for democracy are urgent issues.Others, however, are crucial:For example, if there isn't a pro-democracy movement that works together and includes everyone, all of the efforts to raise accountability and change the rules of what is legal and acceptable will be seen as partisan, and most of them will fail or even worsen polarization.

The ill effects of the decline in American democracy will not be limited to the country's borders.Stumbles in American democracy severely harm democracy abroad as autocratic coordination grows.A significant setback to U.S. democracy would have enormous effects on global poverty and well-being due to the strong correlations between democracy and economic growth through improved human capital, peace, and even life expectancy.

The stakes are very high, and the polarization that is making these issues harder to fix gets stronger with each passing moment.To save our democracy, Americans must begin now, on a large scale, strategically, with a broad cross-party coalition.

Correction:The information that Jeff Flake decided not to run for reelection has been added to the text.Additionally, Boebert, Greene, and Cawthorn were elected in 2020 rather than 2018.